Death Scene Investigation

A FIELD GUIDE

Death Scene Investigation

A FIELD GUIDE

SCOTT A. WAGNER, MD

CRC Press
Taylor & Francis Group
Boca Raton   London   New York

CRC Press is an imprint of the
Taylor & Francis Group, an **informa** business

CRC Press
Taylor & Francis Group
6000 Broken Sound Parkway NW, Suite 300
Boca Raton, FL 33487-2742

© 2009 by Taylor & Francis Group, LLC
CRC Press is an imprint of Taylor & Francis Group, an Informa business

No claim to original U.S. Government works
Printed in the United States of America on acid-free paper
10 9 8 7 6 5 4 3 2 1

International Standard Book Number-13: 978-1-4200-8676-8 (Softcover)

Library of Congress Cataloging-in-Publication Data

Wagner, Scott.
  Death scene investigation : a field guide / Scott A. Wagner.
     p. ; cm.
  Includes bibliographical references and index.
  ISBN 978-1-4200-8676-8 (alk. paper)
  1. Forensic pathology. 2. Death--Causes. 3. Autopsy. I. Title.
     [DNLM: 1. Forensic Medicine--methods. 2. Autopsy--standards. W 800
  W135d 2008]

  RA1063.4.W32 2008
  614'.1--dc22   2008040361

**Visit the Taylor & Francis Web site at
http://www.taylorandfrancis.com**

**and the CRC Press Web site at
http://www.crcpress.com**

Dedication

This book is dedicated to the memory of Phyllis Wagner

Contents

4   Detailed Physical Assessment of the Body at the Scene   29

5   The Medical History and Medical Records   39

6   Natural Diseases and Death Investigation   45

7   Traumatic Injuries   67

8   Identification Methods   111

9   Signs of Cardiopulmonary Resuscitation and Treatment   121

10   Signs of Previous Surgeries and Procedures   125

11   The Medical-Legal Autopsy   127

12   Forensic Experts 185

Preface

Death Investigation is an art that is never mastered. It is the fusion of science, old-fashioned footwork, and intuition. Each death scene is unique in some way and presents new challenges to even the most seasoned investigator among us. Even more, long or late hours, unpleasant environmental conditions, and difficult psychosocial situations further complicate the job. It is during those tough times when having and following a protocol pays off. Death investigation scenarios can vary widely but protocols are the tool to keep the results consistent. Skirting protocols for convenience or other reasons can lead to erroneous conclusions — or worse, lost convictions.

During the entire death investigation, from initial call to final courtroom testimony, the *way* things are done is as important as *what* is done. Having and following a standard routine for death investigation minimizes potential errors. Having the appropriate resources and tools at hand to make the job easier and more efficient is also important. Through the course of his or her work, the death investigator must interface with law enforcement, district attorneys, defense attorneys, families, friends, witnesses, medical professionals, media, and countless others in the community. Producing a death investigator's handbook for all situations, in all jurisdictions, is not possible. We seek here to provide a book that is a useful tool for the death investigator with at least some basic training.

Because the majority of deaths in any medical examiner's or coroner's office are natural, emphasis is placed in this area. Death investigators come from varying backgrounds. Those from nonmedical fields will find the drug and disease section useful. Medical terms are often really a "second language," and the words can have odd spellings. The book aims to be a field guide for basic medical information. For those without forensic backgrounds, the forensic glossary can be of use. Words have specific meanings in forensic pathology. The current usage and meaning of these words are given.

Many deaths, usually natural, do not require scene visits, especially those that occur in health-care facilities. The death investigator's role is slightly different in these cases, usually requiring discussions with medical personnel and obtaining medical records. A fair portion of this book also deals with handling medical information.

Finally, because the book is a field guide, it will not answer all questions raised. However, references are supplied for seeking further information when one gets back to the office. For the death investigator, knowing where to look for an answer is more important than memorizing a great deal of data.

It is my intention that the information and images in this book be used only by the professionals and students in the fields of or related to death scene investigation, law enforcement, death investigation, and law, or by funeral directors. Improper uses of these images can be a violation of the law, and using these photographs in a salacious manner violates the basic ethics the author and his colleagues uphold. The first lesson to learn in death scene investigation is reverence for the deceased and their families. In keeping with this reverence, we honor the deceased by using the information learned to study diseases and injuries for the benefit of the living.

Scott A. Wagner, M.D.

Acknowledgments

The author would like to thank the estate of Jay Dix, M.D., for permission to use the medical technology, diagrams, and drug sections of this book. Dr. Dix's book, *Handbook for Death Scene Investigators,* was a strong influence for both the idea and format of this book. Thanks to Robert Gutekunst, M.D., for proofreading the manuscript and providing suggestions. Others essential to the success of this book include Alexis Rodriguez, for research on Web sites; Dick Alfeld for fielding questions; and my teachers for the inspiration. Amanda and Natalie, thanks for understanding.

Guidelines for the Death Scene Investigator

1

Purpose of the Death Investigation

Although the primary goal of a death investigation is to establish the cause and manner of death, the role of the investigator extends much further than simply answering these two questions. A common question asked is, "Why does it matter? The person is dead." While it is true that the dead cannot benefit, the value in death investigation is to benefit the living and future generations. In a culture that values life, explaining the death in a public forum (the meaning of "forensic") is crucial for many reasons. And this interest goes beyond simple curiosity. Listed below are some common reasons that death investigations are performed for the benefit of all living persons.

Death investigation benefits include:

1. Families of the deceased:
   - Discover genetic/inherited disorders
   - Collection of death benefits, e.g., life insurance, black lung funds
   - Answer questions about the death, e.g., "why did he complain of headaches?"
   - Psychological benefit of knowing the truth, peace of mind
2. Legal systems, civil and criminal:
   - Provide evidence for prosecution in a criminal matter causing death (e.g., murder, manslaughter, neglect of a dependant causing death, etc.)
   - Provide evidence to exonerate a person under suspicion
   - Provide evidence for civil matters, such as negligence causing death
   - Death of a person in custody
3. Public health and safety:
   - Identify infectious diseases, both new and old

- Identify defective devices or products that can cause death
- Identify trends in deaths to develop strategies for the future (e.g., sudden infant death syndrome [SIDS] death rate)

4. Medical care quality:
   - May be conducted within the hospital or institution or by the medical examiner or coroner
   - Evaluation of the effectiveness of treatments and therapy
   - Evaluation of the potential errors of individuals or the system
   - Evaluation of transplant donors for signs of disease or injuries that might affect the transplant recipient
   - Research (e.g., to evaluate the adverse effects of a novel drug or therapy)

Role of the Death Scene Investigator (DSI)

The death scene investigator (DSI) is a coroner, medical examiner, or a death investigator charged by the federal government, state, county, parish, or municipality with conducting death investigations. The death investigator commonly works under the direction of the medical examiner or coroner.

Death investigation is accomplished by the interaction of many individuals with varying expertise. Often, the DSI coordinates many of the activities, agencies, and final outcomes regarding the death. The families and loved ones of the deceased often have many questions about how the person died. Law enforcement and prosecution need the investigator's input. Environmental challenges such as noting the cherry-red lividity of carbon monoxide poisoning might only be recognized by the DSI, thus saving the lives of others who might inhabit the building with a faulty furnace. And finally, the pathologist will have questions at the autopsy, as a part of a complete investigation. The investigator is the central hub in the continually turning wheel of death investigation and its subsequent resolution.

Death investigators come from many different backgrounds, which often include law enforcement, medical, funeral directors, and even the clergy. Many investigators bring their past experiences to the field of death investigation and are then trained on the job. There are many training programs available, but few uniform, nationally recognized standards. The American Board of Medicolegal Death Investigators (ABMDI) was founded in the late 1990s to develop a standard training curriculum. Some death investigators are required to obtain this certification.

Philosophy of Death Investigation

In death investigation, the body is the most important piece of evidence. The investigation involves focusing on the body and the attached trace evidence. In forensic pathology, it is often stated that one "takes the victim as he finds him." This axiom simply means that no assumptions are made, and the investigation starts with the body, examining the injuries, diseases, and evidence present to arrive at a cause or manner of death. Observations become facts. When sufficient facts are available, an opinion can be formed. If new facts become available, the opinion can change.

Notification of a Death

The wheels are set in motion by the first call of a death to the coroner's or medical examiner's office. These calls are usually received from law enforcement dispatch, but can originate from health-care facilities, first responders, or funeral homes and other agencies. Having received the notification, the investigation can take on various forms and depths of inquiry depending on the type of death and the circumstances. Taking the initial call, it is important to know if the case is under one's jurisdiction. Below is a list of cases that fall under the jurisdiction of the coroner or medical examiner in many states. Please note that most any death, if suspicious, can come into one's jurisdiction. Generally, jurisdiction over a death is determined by the county in which the death occurred. Exceptions to this would include a death on a ship or airliner, where the jurisdiction would be the nearest port or the airport where the plane lands. Check protocols and medical examiner or coroner laws in your area for details.

In many states, any individual who has knowledge of a suspicious or unnatural death is expected, by law, to report this. Each state has its own state autopsy laws, state anatomy laws, or postmortem examination laws. Deaths that are commonly reported to a medical examiner or coroner are as follows:

- Deaths under unexplained, unusual, suspicious, or unnatural circumstances
- Homicides
- Deaths due to accident, even when the accident does not appear to be the primary cause of death
- Poisoning deaths
- Deaths in which there is no attending physician, or the deceased has not seen a physician recently (30 to 120 days)

- Deaths in which a physician will not sign the death certificate
- Deaths from infectious disease that pose a potential public health risk
- Maternal deaths from abortion
- Stillborn fetus 20 weeks or older whose death was not attended by a medical practitioner
- Death of an inmate or a person in custody
- Deaths during surgery or in proximity of a diagnostic or therapeutic procedure
- Deaths related to a disease or injury acquired or potentially acquired at work
- Sudden unexpected death of a person who suffered a fracture in the past 6 months
- Deaths of organ and transplant donors
- Death of a child, less than 14 years, in which at least two physicians will not sign the death certificate
- Any death in which there is doubt about reporting, should be discussed with the medical examiner/coroner's office (MEC)

The duties of the DSI take him or her to many different places and facilities in the community. The DSI will encounter all types of death cases — from homicides to natural deaths. The following is a summary of the scope of cases commonly encountered by the DSI:

- Medical facility deaths of persons with previously known lethal disease, in which the physician will sign the death certificate
- Home or hospice deaths of persons with previously known lethal disease in which the physician will sign the death certificate
- Medical facility deaths where injury occurred in the facility (e.g., a fall or death during surgery)
- Medical facility deaths where an injured person was taken to the facility (e.g., initially survived gunshot wound of the head)
- Deaths of unknown cause that occur at home
- Deaths involving a motor vehicle
- Deaths in custody
- Deaths in the workplace
- Suspicious deaths or homicides at any location
- Mass fatalities (airliner, train, subway)
- Airplane crash fatalities (smaller aircraft)
- Suicides at the home
- Alleged suicides away from the home

It is the duty of the DSI to obtain crucial data regarding the demographics of a given case. Many find it easy to obtain this information as early as possible in the death investigation. Each MEC office has its own set of demographic data to be collected. Below is a sample listing of important demographic data that can be important in a death investigation:

- Full name of decedent, including at least the middle initial
- Maiden name (if applicable)
- Sex, race, age, and date of birth
- Social security number (for future social security fraud investigations)
- Address of residence, including city, state, and zip code
- Marital status: single (never married) , married, divorced, and widowed
- Home phone and/or cell phone number
- Next-of-kin contact: relationship to deceased, name, address, and telephone number
- Date, location, and time of notification of next-of-kin and by whom
- Employment history; position, name, address, telephone number of company, supervisor's name, and current status (retired, employed, laid off)

No two death investigations will be exactly alike, but all have similar steps that are taken during the initial call, investigation, and resolution. These steps are as follows.

Discovery of Deceased

Determine who made the call and how your agency was contacted.

1. Intake — initial contact:
   - Determine depth of agency involvement (can vary from phone interview to scene visit).
   - Establish phone contact with the scene.
   - Determine jurisdiction.
   - Determine the scope of your agency's responsibility.
   - Do other agencies need to be notified? (e.g., the National Transportation Safety Board [NTSB], Occupational Safety and Health Administration [OSHA], etc.)
2. Information gathering:
   - Identify potential health hazards at the scene (e.g., carbon monoxide [CO], explosions, electrical).
   - Determine the circumstances of death (the story leading up to the death).
   - Collect demographic data, death event data, medical history, criminal history.

- Speak to family, first responders, medical providers, and witnesses.
- Coordinate with evidence technicians in crime scene cases.

3. Initial assessment at the scene:
   - Secure the scene and establish a perimeter.
   - Identify the law enforcement officer in charge (if any).
   - What is the working cause and manner of death?
   - Will an autopsy be needed?
   - Are any additional experts needed at the scene or at the autopsy?

4. Examination of the body, the most important evidence at the scene:
   - Obtain photographic documentation.
   - Obtain a scene diagram.
   - Note scene temperature and conditions.
   - Assess the signs of death: rigor, algor, and livor mortis, and decomposition.
   - Package the body and transport.
   - Postmortem examination, including autopsy.

5. Follow-up information:
   - Toxicology.
   - Autopsy report.
   - Final law enforcement reports.
   - Further investigation.

6. Final report and disposition of case

7. Depositions and trial

The Body and the Scene

2

Statutory Responsibilities

The medical examiner/coroner (MEC) has the statutory responsibility and legal responsibility to determine the cause and manner of death. At most death scenes, because they are natural deaths, this means the MEC has authority and control of the death scene, especially the body. At scenes where law enforcement is present, the scene usually belongs to that agency, but the body is the responsibility of the MEC. At times, especially in high-profile cases and/or homicides, other agencies such as law enforcement and the prosecutor/district attorney will be very interested in collecting evidence if a crime has been committed. Law enforcement usually has control of the scene and evidence.

It is very important that all agencies work together in these situations because there is a common goal, namely that of discovering the facts of the death and the alleged crime. The death scene investigator (DSI) should find and identify himself or herself to the law enforcement personnel in charge. If the MEC clearly has jurisdiction but there is a dispute, it can be useful for the DSI to carry a copy of the appropriate statute to demonstrate authority to those persons doubting it.

Confirm or Validate the Death

Before the death investigation can begin, the death must be officially confirmed. If any signs of life are seen by the first responders, the body will likely not be at the scene and death will be pronounced at the medical facility. In some cases, emergency services will have checked for signs of life and already confirmed the death. Authority to pronounce death varies by state laws. Typically, a physician, MEC, or nurse (under a physician's direction) can pronounce death. Official pronouncement of death is needed to certify the death, and has more practical uses such as estimating the time of death. The time, location, date, and person making the pronouncement of death should be noted by the DSI.

The DSI can occasionally be called to a death scene where he or she must check for signs of life. Signs of death include loss of pulse, respiration, fixed and dilated pupils, and the lack of a blink reflex when touching the eye. More convincing signs of death include algor mortis (loss of heat), rigor mortis (stiffening), livor mortis (settling of blood), and decomposition. The neck can be palpated by the fingers (not the thumb) to check the carotid pulse and the eye can be touched by a cotton swab to confirm the death when the death is thought to be recent.

Securing the Death Scene

In cases where a crime has been committed, or is suspected, the scene will commonly be secured by law enforcement (often the first responding officer) once the victim is confirmed dead. The body might have even been removed from the scene by emergency medical services. The key to securing a crime scene is to preserve and protect all the evidence within, including the body. A reasonable perimeter should be established to encompass this evidence. The DSI should double-check the perimeter on arrival to ensure all evidence is protected. It is much easier to shrink a large perimeter later than it is to deal with contaminated evidence.

In deaths where law enforcement has no presence, such as apparent natural deaths, there is at least an immediate death scene — near the location of the body. The family should be removed from this immediate area because the body must be examined for the signs of death. Also, if criminal charges are the end result, having the family or unauthorized persons at the scene would constitute evidence contamination. In the rare event that such an investigation becomes criminal or suspicious while the scene is being investigated, law enforcement should be contacted and the perimeter expanded. Theoretically, each death is suspicious until evaluated but it is impractical to treat each scene as a homicide scene.

The investigator must formulate a working opinion of the nature of the case so that an appropriate perimeter can be established. Once unauthorized individuals are removed, a perimeter can be established. In fires or cases involving hazardous materials, the scene should only be entered after approval from fire or HAZMAT (HAZardous MATerials) officials. A perimeter can be easy to establish if indoors because a door can be shut, or a portion of a building can be isolated. Outdoor scenes can be complicated to establish, particularly in busy areas. In busy outdoor areas, a generous perimeter should be established so that onlookers, media, and witnesses cannot view or photograph the investigation. Large perimeters are manned by law enforcement personnel controlling who enters and leaves the scene. A scene log sheet is maintained, recording names, the times of entering and leaving the scene, and the agency.

Evidence at the Death Scene

The body is the most important, and often the largest piece of evidence at a death scene. The evidence or crime scene technician at the scene is usually the principal evidence collector, although any law enforcement personnel might also collect evidence. The DSI might collect evidence on the body that could be lost in transport. Evidence from the perpetrator might have transferred to the deceased. This item might be a small hair or nail fragment. At times it is useful to collect these items at the scene, because small items can be easily lost in transport. Evidence should not be touched or removed without the permission of the investigating officer in charge. Any other evidentiary items such as clothing should remain on the body for collection at the morgue, which affords better lighting and a controlled environment in which to collect evidence attached to the body.

Documentation of the Scene and the Body

Documentation by Photography

The camera is an essential tool of the death investigation. To use a photograph in court, it must be a *true and accurate representation* of what the investigator views at the scene. The DSI should have access to a digital camera and, at a minimum, know how to use the basic features. While many jurisdictions employ technicians to perform standard crime scene photography, there are numerous reasons the DSI will find the digital camera likely the most useful tool in his or her bag. At smaller scenes, the DSI might be the only individual with a camera. Also, MEC offices often desire a second set of pictures, focused on the body and the evidence connected to the body. Many investigators find that having digital images handy can assist in report writing by aiding in remembering significant details.

Uses of digital photography include:

- Provides a true and accurate representation of observations
- Documents the positions of evidence and the body
- Documents the steps of removal of evidence and the body
- Allows immediate review of the photograph's quality

- Refreshes the memory, days or even years later
- Allows experts, colleagues, and jurors to review the evidence
- Digital format allows ease of enlarging the image
- Ease of storage and sharing of digital images

Focusing on the body, the DSI should tell a photographic story about the body at the scene. Photos are begun before any objects are moved. Take overall photos of the relationship of the body to the environment and evidence. Then focus toward the body and evidence around the body. Photos should then be taken depicting all four sides of the body (including the back). When possible, the photographs should be taken at right angles to a body or object, to avoid a *perspective illusion* in the photo. Perspective illusion causes objects in the foreground to appear larger than those in the background when an object is photographed at anything other than a 90° angle. As the photographic documentation proceeds, one should periodically review the photos for quality. Photographing the body at autopsy is covered in Chapter 11.

Polaroid photography is useful for identification photos because the print can be made on the spot and shown to family members. These photos can deteriorate over time, and should be scanned and made into a digital file if long-term storage is needed. Video documentation is another useful tool, especially in complex death scenes. The body, evidence, and other objects can be viewed from multiple angles. Because a video consists of 30 frames per second, the mind assembles this group of images into a three-dimensional view of the object. Also, by panning and zooming in and out, a video can provide a perspective of the scene and body location that is difficult to match with still photography. Digital video is widely available and easily stored.

In any type of visual identification, be it photos or videos, one should generally avoid shots of an investigator performing a task. Investigators are neither actors nor are they accustomed to appearing on camera. Camera angles, shadows, and perspective artifacts can distort the facts and detract from the main goal of visual documentation — to provide a *true and accurate representation* of the facts.

Many investigators keep a photo log, recording the location, date, condition, case number, photo number, and notes about the photos. Photos should be made with some type of designation of the date and time the photos are logged. This can be accomplished simply by burning the files to a compact disc, and signing and dating the disc. Many programs automatically designate the time a photo was taken and the date modified. In any event, these steps will allow the investigator to demonstrate that the photos were not altered after being taken.

Documentation by Diagrams

In addition to images, diagrammatic documentation adds additional views of the scene that aid in understanding the location of the body at the scene. Commonly, the scene is sketched with major fixed physical objects in place, such as walls or fence posts. Indoors, the diagrams look like a rough floor plan of a house or building. Outdoors, compass readings and Global Positioning System (GPS) coordinates are used. In the *coordinate method*, the body is measured from at least two fixed objects (points of reference) and a part on the body (usually the head). Outdoors, the triangulation method is used, measuring the body's relationship to three or more widely spaced reference points. The diagram contains essential information such as the body and the murder weapon, but not all objects found at the scene. The diagram should have the preparer's name, date, exact location (including compass direction and GPS coordinates in some cases), case number, and the name of anyone assisting. Unless the diagram is to scale, one should indicate, "Not drawn to scale" on the diagram.

Forming Preliminary Opinions: Be Suspicious but Objective

Upon receiving the first call to and information about a death scene, the DSI should formulate a working opinion about the nature of the case so that the proper resources are at the scene. Opinions are based on facts and as information is gathered, the facts can change. One should not be close-minded at any time — that is, drawing a conclusion before all the information is available. Committing to a firm opinion too early in the investigation will stop objectivity. If the death investigator becomes biased and loses objectivity, this will show up in the conclusions of the investigation and even on the witness stand. The DSI often finds evidence that may exonerate one suspect and incriminate another.

The burden of proof is on the prosecution in criminal cases. For the death investigation team, this means that enough evidence is collected in a criminal case to prove guilt in a court of law beyond a reasonable doubt. Homicide, and suicide and accidents for that matter, must be *proven* to the standard of *reasonable scientific probability* or *reasonable medical certainty*. However, the DSI must be suspicious and objective at the same time. The DSI is not law enforcement. The detectives have a different role, which is to find probable cause to arrest a suspect and assemble a motive and *corpus delicti* ("body of the crime"). The DSI should not try to do the detective's job, but provide objective analysis of the evidence and information for the detective and other members of the prosecution team.

The role of the DSI is to find truthful, objective answers to the questions surrounding the death. One only has one first chance at the scene, and the information is easier to get and can be more accurate early in the investigation. Pertinent questions to be posed at the death scene include:

- Identity and home address of the deceased
- Reason the person is at the location at the time of death. Does the person belong there? (e.g., a person at a stranger's house)
- Is the person dressed appropriately for the scene? (e.g., shorts and a T-shirt outside in winter)
- Begin investigating the person's background and medical history. Ask friends and family. If at a home, review files, business cards, medication bottles, etc.
- Begin to form a range of the time of death. When was the last time the mail or the newspaper was picked up? When was the person last seen or spoken to? Check cell or home phone. Check for the signs of death (see Chapter 3)
- Perform a cursory examination of the body.
- Is this the only scene? Has the body been moved? Has the scene been altered or sanitized? For example, if fingernails are missing from the fingers and are not at the scene, this could be a second or a sanitized scene (see Figure 2.1).
- Is the body position appropriate for the scene? Inappropriate livor or rigor indicates that the body has been moved (see Figure 2.2).
- How does the environment factor into the death and state of the body? For example, multiple deaths in a house in the winter could mean carbon monoxide poisoning. If the body is on a heat register, this could speed decomposition.

Figure 2.1 Broken fingernail from a homicide victim. The broken nail was found at a second crime scene, where the victim was most likely assaulted. Finding and matching this missing nail implicated a suspect in this strangulation homicide.

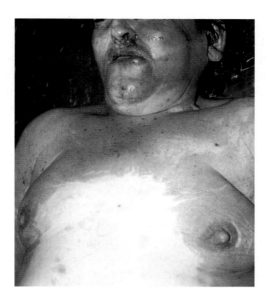

Figure 2.2 Anterior livor mortis. Cleared livor mortis on the front of the body and the folded arms indicate that this body was found face-down and turned over.

Examination of the Body at the Scene

After the body and the surrounding evidence have been documented, the body can be examined. The steps in examining the body at the scene can be summarized as follows:

1. Note the location, conditions, wind speed and direction, temperature, and humidity.
2. Note significant environmental facts (e.g., body on a heat register).
3. Check given sex, weight, and height against direct observation of the body. Driver's license and other forms of ID are often inaccurate.
4. Starting where the body lies, examine from head to toe (preferably prone, or front of body facing up). This exam should be repeated after the body is moved if the body was in an awkward or contorted position.
5. Remove any trace evidence that could be lost in transport. In most cases, evidence on the body should remain there until the autopsy.
6. Do not undress the body at the scene or remove any medical devices from resuscitation.
7. Begin scene assessment of the body (see Chapter 3).
8. Assess rigor, livor, and algor mortis as well as decomposition (see Chapter 3).
9. Evaluate for signs of trauma and disease.
10. Be sure to photo-document the body before, during, and after the exam.

11. Note any significant findings or questions and discuss them with the pathologist at the autopsy.
12. Prepare the body for movement by bagging the hands (and head as some prefer) and by wrapping the body in a clean white sheet.
13. DO NOT allow the body to be transported face down. This can cause livor to fix in the face, as well as "smashing" the face and nose.

Pathologist's Role at the Scene

The DSI is often the most knowledgeable person at the scene regarding the body and the findings on the body. In some deaths, the situation is complex or out of the DSI's scope of expertise. At other times, it simply helps to have another pair of eyes. In unusual or high-profile cases, the pathologist often prefers to view the body at the scene firsthand. Many MEC offices have guidelines for summoning a pathologist to a scene, as large offices have the manpower to have a pathologist go to many death scenes. Below is a list of the types of situations in which it is useful to call the pathologist to the scene:

- Blunt force injury homicides (the pathologist might identify the murder weapon)
- High-profile cases
- Multiple-death cases
- Unusual or bizarre deaths and homicides (see Figure 2.3)

Figure 2.3 Unusual death scenes. When the scene is bizarre or unusual, it often benefits the investigation to summon the pathologist so he or she can view the scene firsthand. Most MEC offices have criteria for summoning a pathologist to the scene.

- Serial homicides
- Homicides or suicides where law enforcement or prosecution requests a pathologist
- Hit-and-run traffic deaths
- Deaths where the time of death is at issue
- Cases where the investigator is uncertain

Other Forensic Experts at the Scene

Anthropologists, entomologists, botanists, and other experts often prefer to be at the scene to collect their own evidence. In many areas, these experts are not close by, but might be available by phone to assist in the proper collection of evidence. The DSI should keep the contact information of these experts close at hand for quick reference.

Assessment of the Body at the Scene

3

Position of the Body at the Scene

Victims may be found in contorted or apparently uncomfortable positions on the floor, commonly the bedroom or bathroom. Generally, the more contorted the body, the more sudden the death. The person appears to have "fallen in his tracks." However, this does not mean the decedent lying apparently comfortably in bed did not also die suddenly. Bodies found in awkward positions that compromise breathing can die of positional asphyxia. The chest wall must be able to rise and fall for respiration to occur. If one is wedged too tightly in a position, the chest wall cannot rise and fall.

A common misconception among laypeople is that a "painful" expression on the face or a contorted position means the person suffered during the process of dying. Generally, there is no correlation between facial expressions, body positions, and suffering. Pain and suffering can be assessed before and during the dying process, but it is done carefully and generally by the pathologist after evaluating the autopsy and investigative information. This information can be useful to the family, and can become arguable in civil court cases.

Blood at the Scene

Both natural and unnatural deaths can produce abundant blood at a scene. Traumatic deaths that involve arterial or venous bleeding, such as stabbing, can produce abundant blood at the scene with spattering. Gunshot wounds can cause extensive external bleeding, but some wounds can cause minimal external bleeding and massive internal bleeding. In short, the amount of blood perceived at a scene does not indicate the severity of the trauma.

Blood spattering at the scene usually indicates trauma, especially if the spatter is high on the walls or on the ceiling. The spatter should be photographed and shown to blood spatter experts if needed.

Certain natural deaths can produce abundant blood at a scene, mimicking a violent death. Alcoholics can bleed from varices in the esophagus. The varices are dilated blood vessels produced when blood travels around the liver, hardened by cirrhosis. Stomach ulcers can cause fatal bleeding. Lung tumors or tuberculosis can produce bleeding from the lung. This bleeding can be quite extensive and blood can be seen in the toilet, bathtub, towels, and sinks. Even severe nosebleeds can cause a fatality under the right conditions.

At times, other fluids can be mistaken for blood, such as the purged fluid that exudes from the mouth and nose in decomposing bodies. This fluid is brown and malodorous. Any doubts about the fluid can be answered at the autopsy.

Vomitus at the Scene

One common problem in the investigation of sudden death is the interpretation of the presence of vomitus on the face. Many investigators have learned incorrectly that the presence of vomitus indicates that the deceased aspirated or choked on the vomitus, and that this represents the cause of death. Vomiting is often an involuntary action that is present in deaths of many causes. Vomitus contains acid powerful enough to cause chemical burns on the face, making it appear that a caustic chemical had been ingested. Aspiration of large amounts of vomitus material can cause death, and if the person initially survives, can develop severe pneumonia, which can be fatal as well. The goal of the investigation is to find the cause of the vomiting, which will aid in finding the cause and the manner of death.

Vomitus is routinely seen in a number of deaths (which the author calls "terminal vomiting"), including deaths involving profound unconsciousness, such as drug- or alcohol-induced coma and brain injury or disease. Cardiac deaths often produce vomiting. In fact, virtually any death can produce vomiting, likely because there is a period of profound loss of consciousness and loss of neuronal control of visceral reflexes. Noting vomitus in multiple locations around the scene can be an indication of an illness causing vomiting, rather than terminal vomiting.

Physical Examination of the Body at the Scene

The Scene Assessment

The body is assessed or examined head to toe at the scene. The aim of this examination is to gain some insight into the nature of the death. Wounds can be blood covered and the lighting poor, so firm conclusions cannot be drawn from this exam. Keep in mind that an autopsy will likely be performed. If an autopsy is not eventually performed, a more detailed examination should be made at another facility, such as the morgue, where the body can be undressed, the lighting is better, and the environment is more controlled.

A scene assessment of the body can provide law enforcement and others of the death investigation team with a working cause of death, or at least several possibilities. It should be made clear that this information is *preliminary and subject to a full autopsy and further investigation*. Often, the death scene investigator (DSI) is the most knowledgeable person at the scene in determining the cause of death. Any conclusions the DSI makes after a scene investigation can be taken literally, so caution is advised here: make it clear that *all opinions are working opinions*!

Starting the Scene Assessment of the Body and Time of Death

When first touching the body, the four signs of death should be evaluated because once the body is moved, the rigor mortis will be changed or "broken." After rigor, algor, and livor mortis are assessed, the remainder of the scene assessment of the body can begin.

The determination of time of death, or the interval between the time of death and when the body is found (i.e., *postmortem interval*), can only be estimated unless there is a credible witness or a watch breaks and freezes the time of the traumatic incident. The longer the time since death, the greater the chance one has for error in determining the postmortem interval. There are numerous individual observations using the body and investigative information that, when used together, provide the best estimate of the time of death. To create the best estimate of the postmortem interval, the examiner must check the following: rigor mortis, livor mortis, body temperature, and decompositional changes. A thorough scene investigation is necessary. The scene environment is the single most important factor in determining the postmortem interval. *Keep in mind that in most cases, the postmortem interval is only a best estimate of the time of death, for which only a range of times can be given.*

Rigor Mortis

Rigor mortis literally means "the stiffening of death." It is a chemical reaction in which a stable complex of adenosine and myosin of the muscle fibers causes stiffening in a flexion position (bent). It is a chemical reaction that comes and goes. In checking for rigor, the jaw, arms, and then the legs are straightened out of the flexion position and the resistance is assessed. Rigor mortis is typically reported as:

- Not yet present
- Beginning in the jaw
- Beginning in the extremities
- Full rigor
- Beginning to dissipate
- No longer present

Because rigor mortis is a chemical reaction, there are many variables on the rate of formation depending on the environment, the size of the person, and the condition of the person at death. Other rigor mortis facts include:

- Muscles begin to stiffen within 1 to 3 hours after death at 70 to 75°F, developing fully after 9 to 12 hours.
- A high fever or high environmental temperature will cause rigor to occur sooner.
- Rigor mortis will occur more quickly if the decedent was involved in strenuous physical activity just before death.
- Rigor mortis is detected first in the jaw, face, upper and lower extremities, in that order. The examiner must check the jaw, then the arms, and finally the legs to feel if the associated joints are moveable.
- The body is said to be in complete (full) rigor when the jaw, elbow, and knee joints are immovable. This takes approximately 9 to 12 hours at 70 to 75°F environmental temperature.
- The body will remain stiff for 24 and up to 36 hours at 70 to 75°F before the muscles begin to loosen, usually in the same order they stiffened.
- Rigor is retarded in cooler temperatures and accelerated in warmer temperatures.
- When the body stiffens, it remains in that position until the rigor passes or the joint is physically moved and the rigor is broken (or decomposition occurs).
- The position of a body in full rigor can give an indication (together with livor) of whether or not a body has been moved after death (see Figure 3.1).

Livor Mortis (Blood Settling)

Livor mortis is the gravity-dependent settling of blood after death. After death, with the stoppage of the heart, gravity takes over and the blood

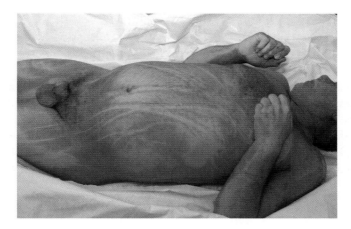

Figure 3.1 The rigor and livor mortis patterns tell a story. This body was found face down on a wrinkled sheet in rigor with the hands up as shown. Turning the body over reveals the arms configured in a flexed position and pressure-cleared livor, including long vertical lines from the wrinkles in the sheet.

settles in the lowest parts of the body. If these areas are pressed, the lividity will clear, or "blanch." Because blood is pigmented, it eventually leaches out of the blood vessels, breaks down (hemolyzes), and then stains the tissues after a period of time (called "fixed lividity"). Livor mortis is recorded as follows:

- Absent
- Blanching in the dependent (down) areas
- Partially fixed in the dependent areas
- Fixed in the dependent areas
- Covering most or all of the body (e.g., bodies found in water)

If a body is moved before lividity is fixed, lividity will shift, causing two patterns. This phenomenon can allow the investigator to detect whether a body has been moved. Intense lividity can be mistaken for contusions by nonexperts. Any questions regarding lividity and contusions can be resolved at autopsy. Lividity does not involve hemorrhage into the skin, as does a contusion. Below are additional facts regarding livor mortis:

- Livor mortis is a purplish-red discoloration in the tissues that can be seen as early as 30 minutes after death, and becomes more visible over time.
- Blood will settle in the blood vessels, then tissues (when "fixed") in the gravity-dependent (lowest) areas of the body.
- Dependent areas that contact the surface that the body is resting on will show "clearing of livor." Also, the bony areas beneath the skin will

compress the skin against the surface and prevent the blood from settling in the tissues (Figure 3.2).

- Livor mortis is noticeable approximately 1 hour after death and becomes
  fixed in about 8 to 10 hours.
- When livor is fixed, the color will not blanch under pressure and will
  remain in those areas even if the body is repositioned.
- Even if the body is moved after lividity is fixed, there may be a slight discoloration in the new dependent areas even though the blood remains
  fixed in the original position.
- Fixed blood seen in a nondependent location indicates that a body has
  been moved after death.
- Livor mortis will be visible until the body becomes completely discol-
  ored by decomposition.
- Carbon monoxide poisoning will cause the livor to be bright red. Cold,
  freezing, refrigeration, and cyanide poisoning causes red-to-salmon-
  pink lividity (Figure 3.3).
- Livor mortis can be more difficult to evaluate in dark-skinned individuals because the color contrast makes the red-purple color difficult
  to see.
- Intense lividity in dependent areas, such as the head or the extremities
  hanging downward, can cause rupture of the capillaries and petechial
  hemorrhages (point-like hemorrhages) (Figure 3.4).

Body Cooling (Algor Mortis)

Algor mortis is the loss of heat after death. Although measuring the loss of
heat of a body is the most common scientific method for estimating the time

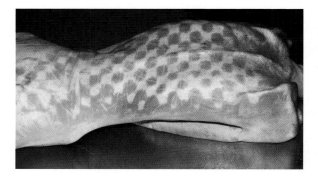

Figure 3.2 Patterned livor mortis. Because livor mortis can be cleared with
pressure, objects pressing against the skin when livor forms can cause a pattern.
This individual was lying on an "eggcrate" foam mattress. The foam tips of the
mattress touch the skin and clear the livor, while the cups of the mattress allow
the livor formation.

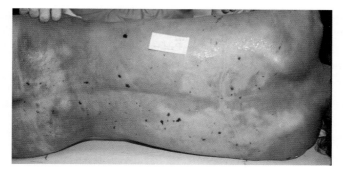

Figure 3.3 Pink lividity can be seen in frozen bodies (as shown above) or in cyanide poisoning.

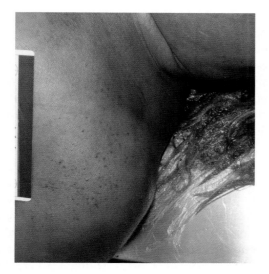

Figure 3.4 Petechiae and livor mortis are seen in the upper body of this victim of suffocation and strangulation because the body was placed upside down after the homicide.

of death, there are many variables further complicating this estimate. Normal temperatures vary widely in individuals. Exercise and fever can raise temperatures. Post mortem, the body does not cool at a linear rate. Body type (mainly the amount of body fat), clothing, and age also change the rate at which a body loses heat.

Measuring postmortem temperatures remains controversial today for the above reasons. Some offices simply use a gloved hand and report the body warm or cold to touch, while some take a rectal or ear temperature. Others make a small incision at the scene and take at least two liver temperatures. Each method has its merits and drawbacks. Reporting warm and cold to touch is subjective and can vary with an individual. It may be impractical to pull down the pants or to incise the abdomen at the scene. The DSI should check local practices for postmortem temperature reporting.

Additional facts regarding algor mortis include:

- After death, the body cools from its normal internal temperature to the surrounding environmental temperature.
- Measuring body cooling is not always an accurate method of predicting the postmortem interval.
- At an ideal environmental temperature of 70°F to 75°F, the body cools at approximately 1.5°F per hour in the early postmortem period.
- If a decedent's body temperature was higher than normal because of individual variation, infection, or physical exercise, 98.6°F (37°C) is not an accurate starting point.
- The outside environment determines the rate of cooling. Cooling occurs more quickly in the cold and may occur slowly or not at all in hot climates.
- If body temperature is measured at the scene, it should be taken on at least two separate occasions before the body is moved.
- A rectal or liver temperature is the most accurate measurement.
- The environmental temperature should be recorded.

Eyes

If the eyes remain open after death, the corneas (the central, clear covering over the eye) will become cloudy within 2 to 3 hours. If the eyes are closed, cloudiness might take up to 24 hours. Eyes that remain open in a dry environment will become blackened in the sclera (i.e., covering over the whites of the eyes). This is called *tâche noire* ("black drying"), and can be mistaken for bruising.

Clothing

The type of clothing may help indicate what the person was doing and the time of day at death. The type of clothing should be correlated with the person's schedule and habits. For example, if one finds a man in pajamas who worked third shift and slept during the day, this would have a different meaning than a first-shift employee who slept at night. This information should be used with caution and as a guideline because one's attire can vary widely. Thick clothing will hold heat in the body, potentially changing postmortem heat loss.

Determining Time of Death by Scene Investigation

Information from the scene, other than that associated with the body, may also be critical in estimating the time of death. All clues from a house or an apartment must be analyzed. Was the mail picked up? Were the lights on or off? Was food being prepared? Were any major appliances on? Was there any indication as to the kind of activity the individual was performing, had completed, or was contemplating? How was the person dressed? What do the witnesses say about the person's habits? When was the last time the person was known to be alive? Was the phone used? These questions allow the DSI to "climb inside" the deceased in the scene environment to understand what the deceased was doing just before death.

Forensic Entomology and Time of Death

Insect larvae and other insects associated with the body can be used to estimate the postmortem interval. An entomologist will be able to determine not only the type of larvae, but also its developmental stage. From egg to adult insect, each stage has a specific time duration that enables an entomologist to state how long the insects have been present (Figure 3.5). The species of insect present and the habits of the insect are also important; for example, carrion beetles prefer decaying material. Remember that this time estimate is based only on the time that larvae were present on the body.

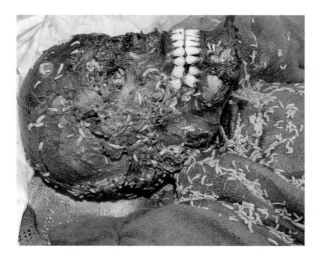

Figure 3.5 Fly larvae. Forensic entomologists are very effective, using the time for fly larva development and other insect data to estimate the postmortem interval.

That is, if a body was moved from indoors to outdoors, the true postmortem interval estimate based on insects will be skewed. Larvae and insects of varying ages can be saved in alcohol or saved live with tissue media. In significant cases where time of death is important, the author recommends contacting and, if possible, summoning a forensic entomologist to the scene.

Beetles, larvae, and other insects can bore into the body and cause holes in the skin that can resemble injuries, such as gunshot wounds. Insects seem to be drawn to areas that are injured, such as a gunshot wound of the face. Exposed areas are also more susceptible to insect activity.

Forensic Botany and Time of Death

Flora discovered under or near the body may be helpful. A botanist may be able to examine the specimen, classify the type of flora and time of year it would normally be present, and determine how much time elapsed to reach that particular growth stage.

Decomposition

Decomposition is the fourth sign of death behind rigor, livor, and algor mortis. Decompositional times can vary widely, depending on the climate. Hot, subtropical areas can produce advanced decomposition in as little as 24 hours, as compared to a northern climate where the same amount of decomposition might take 1 week or longer. Decomposition begins when a musty, rancid odor first appears. Once the investigator smells this, the odor is not easily forgotten. This odor is from processes called autolysis and putrefaction, and the changes are largely due to bacteria from the body breaking down tissue. Decompositional changes then progress from greenish discoloration of the abdomen to skeltonization. The progression of changes during decomposition includes:

1. The first change is a greenish discoloration of the abdomen, and then the discoloration spreads throughout the body.
2. As discoloration occurs, the body will begin to swell due to bacterial gas formation that is promoted in warm weather and retarded in cold weather. Tissues swell and the eyes and tongue protrude.
3. As the body becomes bloated, the epidermis begins to slip and form blisters, and the blood begins to degrade.
4. Degrading blood produces "venous marbling," where hemolyzed blood "tattoos" the tissues, producing outlines of the blood vessels.

5. Purging develops. Decomposed blood and body fluids, appearing dark brown and smelling malodorous, come out of the body orifices, largely due to gas propelling the fluid along the path of least resistance. *This should not be mistaken for blood from an injury.*

6. Finally, skeltonization may take weeks or months, depending on the environment. Many bodies are discovered in partial skeltonization.

7. Exposed portions of the body decompose faster. The visceral part of the body also tends to decompose faster (i.e., abdomen, chest, and head). When a body part is exposed because of injury, that part tends to decompose faster. Insect activity accelerates this decomposition.

8. Decompositional changes depend on temperature, humidity, insect activity, and condition of the body at death (e.g., patients with infections can decompose more rapidly). By way of example, if a person dies at home and the temperature is about 70°F, it is not unusual for the first signs of decompositional changes to appear in 24 to 36 hours.

Other Decompositional Changes

Adipocere

Fat tissue beneath the skin begins to saponify (turn into a white, soapy material), particularly in moist environments. A hard, wax-like material forms, which takes a minimum of a few weeks to develop. Once adipocere forms, the body tends to exist in a relatively preserved state for many months. Unlike normal decompositional changes, there is no green discoloration or significant bloating. The exterior of the body remains white to brown and the outermost layers of the skin slip off.

For bodies totally submerged in cold water, adipocere will be evenly distributed over all body surfaces. Adipocere is not exclusive to bodies found in water. For example, bodies found in plastic bags or wet grave sites, which provide a moist environment, may also undergo this change. There may also be a differential development of adipocere, depending on whether or not areas of the body are clothed.

Mummification

Mummification occurs in hot, dry environments. The body dehydrates and bacterial proliferation may be minimal. The skin becomes dark, dried, and leathery. The process occurs readily in the fingers and toes in dry environments regardless of the temperature. Most mummified bodies are found in

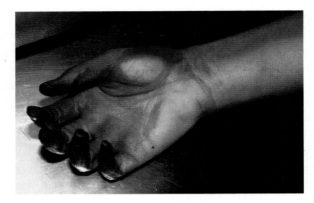

Figure 3.6 Mummification. Hot, dry conditions produce a drying of the tissues, resulting in a dark, leathery appearance. In this case, the fingertips are mummified due to the furnace being turned up to a maximum level by the perpetrator, presumably to speed decomposition. The environmental humidity can be very low under such conditions.

the summer months or in hot, dry climates. Mummification can occur in the winter indoors, especially if the heat is turned up, creating a hot, low-humidity environment (Figure 3.6). It is possible for an entire body to mummify in only a few days to weeks in the right conditions. Once a body is in this state, it can remain preserved for many years.

Detailed Physical Assessment of the Body at the Scene

4

Introduction

The body should be prone (face up) during the examination, if possible. Photos of the original position of the body must be taken before the body is moved. One begins with a general assessment and progresses from head to toe, pushing clothing aside but not removing it. Some find it easier to assess rigor, livor, and algor mortis initially.

The purpose of the assessment of the body at the scene is to provide some insight into the nature of the case and a working cause of death. In many cases, after the signs of death are evaluated, no conclusive information is obtained. At this point, one must wait for the autopsy to gather further information. The findings discussed below can also be noted during an autopsy, which is the best opportunity to perform an examination. In the field, the investigator often has poor lighting conditions, and cannot remove the clothing. The aim of a scene evaluation of the body is to identify findings that will point to information that can be obtained while still at the scene, and the death scene investigator (DSI) can then alert the pathologist to significant findings. At the autopsy, the pathologist will also be looking for the following findings.

Common External Signs of Disease or Trauma

General

- *Unkempt condition:* General uncleanliness such as lack of bathing, very dirty clothes, urine- or feces-stained clothes, long and dirty nails, and poor oral hygiene may be due to alcoholism, drug abuse, or a mental disorder.

- *Condition of the clothing:* The type of clothing may help indicate the time of death and suggest what the person was doing in the perimortem period.
- *Living conditions:* The condition of the apartment or house may give an indication of alcoholism, drug abuse, a mental disorder, severe physical disability, or neglect. Piles of trash, hoarding of items, days to weeks of dirty dishes, urine and feces on the floor, and complete lack of attempts to clean are common scenarios. In the author's experience, one's extreme neglect of hygiene and living conditions is associated with neglect of one's health.
- *Diffuse swelling of the body:* This condition, called *anasarca,* can be seen in kidney failure patients and trauma patients who may have received a great deal of intravenous fluid.
- *Suffusion of livor in the head:* Suffusion of livor mortis in the upper body is marked congestion (blood pooling or "suffusion of livor") of the head, neck, and upper chest (Figure 4.1). Congestion is dark purple and is due to the concentration of blood in these areas. This is an indication that the heart has stopped abruptly, but not immediately. The most common cause is heart disease, especially coronary artery disease; however, any type of heart disease may cause this finding. Other diseases such as seizures, pulmonary thromboemboli (blood clots in the lungs), and asthma, to name a few, can cause this process. Most asphyxial deaths, such as suffocation and a drug overdose, are examples of unnatural deaths causing suffusion of livor.

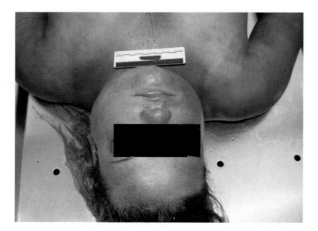

Figure 4.1 Suffusion of livor. Suffusion or congestion of the blood in the upper body, particularly in the head and neck, appears dark purple. This finding is common in asphyxial deaths such as in this case of strangulation, but can be seen in natural deaths such as pulmonary embolus or myocardial infarction.

- *Unequal pupils (anisocoria):* The pupils may be unequal because of head trauma, or may only be an incidental finding because pupil diameter can change after death.
- *Loss of clumps of hair (alopecia):* Alopecia may be seen in natural diseases, such as carcinoma or malnutrition, as well as neglect.
- *Petechiae:* Petechiae are pinpoint hemorrhages, usually of the eyes, eyelids, face, or upper chest. They are due to increased pressure in the capillaries, causing them to rupture. Petechiae of the conjunctiva (eyes) suggest suffocation (see Figure 7.6). Petechiae seen on the face, neck, and chest suggest compressional asphyxia.
- *Poor dentition:* Dental caries (decay) and gingivitis suggest poor medical care, and are seen in chronic alcoholism, drug abuse, or low socioeconomic conditions.
- *Swollen parotid glands:* Parotid glands are on the side of the face, below the cheeks; due to chronic alcoholism.
- *Puffy, round face or "moon face":* Due to long-term steroid use in disease states such as kidney transplant patients, severe arthritis, ulcerative colitis, and some cancer patients.
- *Bright red blood emanating from the nose and/or mouth:* Blood from the nose and mouth often has origins in the upper respiratory tree, mouth, or esophagus from eroded blood vessels, cancer, or alcoholism. Alcoholism can cause cirrhosis of the liver. The liver becomes hard and the blood cannot easily go through the liver, causing the blood to back up in areas such as the esophagus. The blood engorges and distends the veins. These distended veins are called varices. These varices can rupture spontaneously, draining into the mouth or nose, with a high chance of causing death.
- *Blue lips:* Blue lips (or perioral cyanosis) are associated with chronic lack of oxygen (hypoxia) due to heart or lung disease.
- *Sunken eyes:* This finding is usually associated with dehydration, and is also associated with skin tenting (see below). Sunken eyes can also be seen in malnutrition.

Skin

- *Doughlike skin:* In dehydration, the skin loses its moisture and becomes "doughlike." The skin shows "tenting," by not returning to its original position when pulled (Figure 4.2).
- *Jaundice:* Jaundice is a yellowish discoloration of the skin due to an excess of a golden-brown chemical in the body, called *bilirubin.* Jaundice can be seen in liver disease (e.g., hepatitis and liver failure), infection (sepsis), or the rapid breakdown of blood (e.g., if a person receives

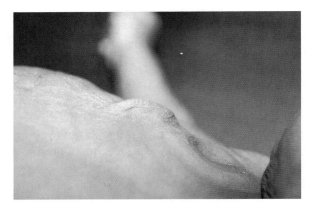

Figure 4.2 "Tenting" of the skin. In dehydration, the tissues appear to be dry and "doughy." Pulling up the skin causes it to "tent" up as the skin tends to remain in the position in which it was pulled.

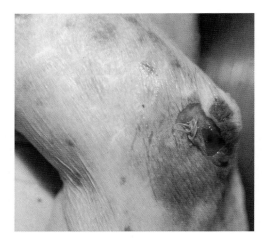

Figure 4.3 Fragile skin with ecchymoses. The elderly, especially when debilitated or malnourished, can have paper-thin skin that tears easily with minor or no apparent trauma. Note the ecchymoses caused by bleeding under the skin, which also is easily caused.

blood of the wrong type). The whites of the eyes (sclera) may be yellow (icterus) and may be the first sign of this process. Many of the tissues, such as the skin, become yellow to golden brown or have that tint.

- *Bruising* (see Chapter 6): A bruise (contusion) is a visual collection of blood in a tissue due to blunt force rupturing the tissue and blood vessels. The elderly bruise more easily due to more fragile tissue (Figure 4.3). Bruises are easier to see in light-skinned individuals. The location and size are very important; for example, a small bruise on the shin may be insignificant, while a large contusion on the face would be of great significance. Significant bruises require further investigation, including an autopsy in most instances.

- *Light areas of skin (hypopigmented areas):* These are either signs of skin disease (loss of pigmentation in dark-skinned individuals called vitiligo) or old trauma, such as healed burns or other serious scars.
- *Brown (pigmented) skin lesions, flat:* These lesions include the benign nevus (mole) and malignant melanoma. Expertise and examination of the lesion under the microscope is needed to determine if the lesion is benign or malignant. Melanoma can be a very aggressive cancer, spreading from the skin to the brain, lungs, and other areas of the body.
- *Raised skin lesions:* Raised skin lesions can be benign or malignant. Benign lesions include cysts, and malignant lesions include cancer that has spread (metastatic), such as in colon or breast cancer.
- *Raised, brown "greasy" lesions:* Seborrheic keratoses are benign moles commonly seen in the elderly (Figure 4.4). If many of these lesions are seen, it can indicate an internal malignancy of the abdomen, particularly the colon.
- *Pale skin:* Extremely pale skin or decreased livor can indicate anemia or blood loss during life.
- *Bleeding into the skin and tissues:* Bleeding into the skin and tissues can arise from poor integrity of the skin or problems related to the clotting of blood, such as patients taking blood thinners (e.g., Coumadin®). Elderly patients can have very thin, papery skin that can tear easily, causing islands of hemorrhage under the skin called

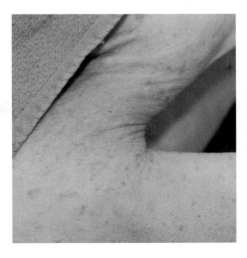

Figure 4.4 Seborrheic keratosis. These brown, greasy-appearing moles are often seen in middle-aged and older people. When these lesions are abundant, internal malignancy should be suspected.

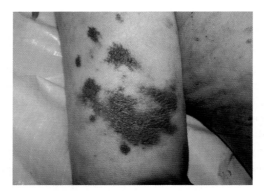

Figure 4.5 Ecchymoses. Ecchymoses are confluent, visible areas of hemorrhage under the skin. These lesions are commonly seen in the very ill or elderly, especially in patients with poor, thin skin or those taking blood thinners such as Coumadin®.

ecchymoses (Figure 4.5). Patients with poor liver function, such as alcoholics, can bleed easily. Before giving an opinion about the severity of bleeding into the skin, the medical condition of the patient should be known.

- *Spider angiomata:* These are small, dilated blood vessels that branch out like spider legs. These lesions can be on the trunk of patients with cirrhosis (e.g., alcoholics) and in other patients without liver disease.

Extremities

- *Cachexia:* Cachexia refers to generalized muscle wastage and a thin, fatless body reminiscent of a starving prisoner or concentration camp victim. This may be seen in any end stage (terminal) chronic disease, such as in a cancer patient. If there is no reason for this appearance, neglect, abuse, and other explanations should be sought, especially when seen in a child or elderly person. Cancer patients can lose lean body mass and develop "cancer cachexia," which is a general wasting-away appearance.
- *Clubbing of the fingers:* This is a rounding and broadening of the fingertips that can be due to lung or congenital heart disease. Clubbed fingers can run in the family as well, which does not indicate disease.
- *Arthritis:* Arthritis means "inflammation of the joints." There are many types of arthritis; however, the most common are osteoarthritis and rheumatoid arthritis. The latter is typified by joint swelling, enlargement, and later, deformity seen especially in the fingers. Look for ulnar deviation (bending of all the fingers toward the little finger) or crooked, twisted fingers.

- *Calves of different sizes:* Reddened, swollen calves can indicate a blood clot in a calf vein (thrombophlebitis). This problem is often seen in patients who have not been mobile. Common medical conditions associated with clots include severe trauma, fractures, major surgery, and any condition that immobilizes a patient. These clots can move up the leg veins, into the heart, then into the lungs (pulmonary embolus). Pulmonary emboli can cause sudden cardiac arrest.

   Pulmonary emboli are known to be a direct complication of a major fracture. If a person falls down the steps accidentally, fractures a hip, and develops a pulmonary embolus, the manner of death is *accident.* This is because the formation of the clot can be traced back to the original injury. If the blood clot formed years later, long after the hip has healed and the patient has been walking around without difficultly, the manner of death is *natural.*
- *Obvious deformities of trunk and limbs:* Loss or deformities of the limbs suggest previous significant trauma. When this situation is encountered, the medical history should be sought. The body always has a story to tell.
- *Swollen ankles (ankle edema):* Puffy, swollen ankles are a common sign in congestive heart failure (CHF) if the patient could walk around or sit. CHF patients confined to bed will have swelling in the lower back (presacral) region. The degree of swelling is judged by the "pitting" of the skin (1+, 2+, or 3+) when pressed by a finger.
- *Loss of hair on the lower legs:* This is usually caused by decreased blood flow from the arteries to the lower legs due to hardening of the arteries (atherosclerosis). This condition is common in smokers and diabetics, and in patients with atherosclerosis elsewhere in the body. The skin becomes very shiny as a result.
- *Brownish discoloration of the lower legs (venous stasis changes):* In the elderly or persons with congestive heart failure (CHF) and other circulatory problems, the veins of the lower legs become congested. Eventually, the veins do not work properly and blood backs up in the tissue, causing a brown discoloration and later, ulcers of the skin (Figure 4.6).
- *Fingernails and toenails:* Aside from examining the nails for forensic evidence (most commonly trace evidence under the nails or broken nails from trauma), the nails can give some clues to disease. Splinter-like hemorrhages under the nails (Figure 4.7) can herald an infection of the heart (subacute bacterial endocarditis). An indentation of the nail (Beau's line) can indicate a severe illness in the previous 6 months (it takes 6 months for a new nail to form). Transverse, white lines in the nail beds (Mees' lines) can be seen in arsenic, thallium, and other poisonings.

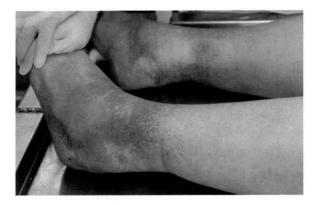

Figure 4.6 Venous stasis changes. Chronic congestion of the blood in the ankle region causes swelling and eventual brownish discoloration of the skin. Such changes are usually due to a combination of heart failure and poor circulation.

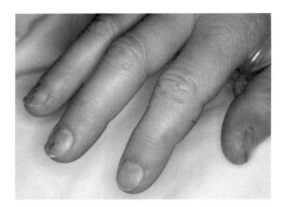

Figure 4.7 Splinter hemorrhages in the nail beds. This figure shows splinter hemorrhages in the middle and ring finger nail beds. This is a sign of bacterial endocarditis and vegetations on the mitral or aortic heart valves. In this condition, small bacteria-laden emboli are disseminated throughout the arterial system into the nail beds, kidneys, and brain.

Trunk

- *Enlarged breasts in men (gynecomastia)*: Alcoholic cirrhosis of the liver causes an increase in estrogen in the body. In men, this can lead to breast tenderness and enlargement. Other causes include marijuana, heroin, drugs for human immune deficiency virus (HIV) treatment, and anabolic steroids used as performance enhancers by athletes.
- *Protuberance ("sticking out") of the abdomen:* This finding must be differentiated from general obesity, air from CPR, air in the abdominal

cavity, and fluid accumulation from disease (e.g., ascites [fluid] in the abdomen due to cirrhosis).

- *Barrel-shaped chest*: This is commonly seen in patients with chronic emphysema.
- *Tense (tight or "tympanic") abdomen:* This is due to accumulated blood or fluid in the peritoneal cavity. It may be from a natural process such as alcoholism, cancer, or trauma.

The Medical History and Medical Records

5

Obtaining a Medical History at the Scene

Because approximately half the deaths that fall under the jurisdiction of the medical examiner/coroner (MEC) are "Manner of death: natural," the death scene investigator (DSI) must be familiar with medical terminology, common diseases and conditions, and the system in his or her jurisdiction to obtain medical records and information. To those investigators without a medical background, it will take some experience, training, study, and help to become efficient at investigating natural deaths.

Investigating natural deaths might not be very exciting to some but can be interesting and rewarding. For example, the author once found an aortic aneurysm in a 14-year-old girl who died suddenly while running. Knowing this condition to be genetic, a study of 12 family members showed the same abnormality in three, thus saving those individuals the same fate as their relative.

Searching the Scene

The scene should be searched for a medical history in nearly all death investigations. This search may be as simple as finding an inhaler for asthma nearby a gunshot wound victim or as complicated as going through cabinets full of medication at a residence. The deceased's physician can always be called and the hospital records will be available tomorrow, but one has only a single chance to explore the scene to find out what is really going on with the person's diseases and treatment. Many people do not take the treatments the doctor ordered and reject advice given at the hospital. Only interviewing witnesses and searching the scene will reveal this information.

Potential sources of information regarding medical history at the scene include:

1. Interview of family and/or neighbors.
2. Searching the house for medications and other medical devices.
3. Searching the house for medical bills and actual medical records.
4. Looking at an address book, cell phone, or documents at home for doctors' names.

The amount of information obtained from a family member can be highly variable. So-called "caretakers" of the family (usually, but not always, the mother or daughter) will have extensive information. Most family members will know about major events and problems such as myocardial infarctions and high blood pressure. Friends and neighbors usually know less but it is always worth asking because some people prefer not to tell family members about illnesses. At times in death investigation, it seems like a common theme is that "he has not seen a doctor in years," and therefore no information is available. However, the same person might know of symptoms the deceased may have had. Any of these individuals should be asked the following questions about the deceased:

- Medical problems and diseases?
- Symptoms (e.g., shortness of breath, chest pains)?
- Medications or therapies (e.g., oxygen)?
- Doctors or other medical professionals?
- Recent hospitalizations?
- Surgeries?

The scene should be searched for medications, medical devices, and medical appliances. Many patients with artificial joints, coronary artery stents, pacemakers, and the like have cards that are made to carry in a wallet or purse. Medication lists can often be found in the wallet or purse. Medication bottles can tell the whole story of a patient's condition (Figure 5.1). Finding heart failure medication, an inhaler, insulin, antibiotics, and home oxygen indicates that the patient had heart failure, severe chronic lung disease with an infection, and diabetes. Also, the treating physician and possibly hospital information can be obtained from the bottles.

Obtaining Medical Records or Information by Phone

When calling a hospital, health-care facility, doctor's office, the DSI should identify the office and jurisdiction he or she is with. Some health-care

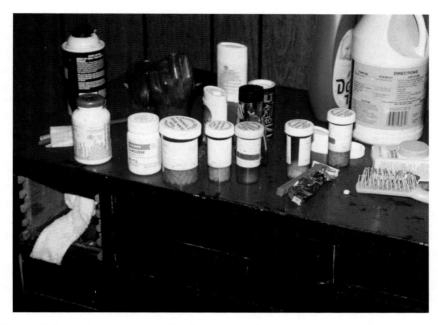

Figure 5.1 Medications at a death scene. The prescription medications at a death scene can tell a story of the medical history of an individual. Diltiazem® and high blood pressure medications indicate ischemic heart disease and hypertension. Theophylline® and other related respiratory medications suggest chronic obstructive lung disease (COLD or COPD), and a recently filled broad-spectrum antibiotic indicates a recent infection.

providers will deny access, citing the HIPAA (Health Insurance Portability and Accountability Act) regulations regarding confidentiality of records. The HIPAA regulations state that coroners and medical examiners are exempt from HIPAA regulations. It can be useful to carry a copy of these regulations to show or fax to a facility that challenges the investigator's authority. See http://www.hipaadvisory.com/regs/standardsprivacyindividid/disclosure medexam.htm or http://www.hhs.gov/ocr/hipaa/ for more information. The MEC should set up an agreement regarding the acquisition of records in advance with the health information supervisors at as many health-care facilities as possible. This understanding will greatly speed up the time it takes to get these records in hand.

The best single source for medical information on a patient is the primary care physician (internist, or gynecologist for women) or family practice physician. Nurse practitioners or nurses working in the office are often a very helpful source. In an ideal situation, the physician remembers the patient well, or remembers the patient after reviewing his or her own office chart. The physician should be asked if he or she is willing to sign the death certificate. Some physicians, for fear of civil liability or other more mysterious reasons, will not be willing to sign the death certificate even though the patient might have a known fatal illness, such as cancer or heart failure. Some physicians, in the author's experience, think that in not signing the death certificate, an autopsy will be performed automatically. The DSI should discuss the reasons a physician might want an autopsy performed in these cases. In any event, as a result of the physician not signing, these cases must be taken by the MEC so that a death certificate can be produced. Many MEC offices will sign the death certificate in such cases without an autopsy after reviewing the medical records.

Physicians and other health-care professionals not familiar with death investigation and forensic pathology might not understand the investigative processes. Physicians might offer proposed causes of death at the hospital. While these opinions are worth noting, autopsy findings can be surprisingly different from the clinical picture, and a ruling on the correct cause of death in many of these cases will occur only after the autopsy.

Hospital death investigation begins with notification of the death by hospital personnel. All health-care facilities in the MEC's jurisdiction should have specific criteria for calling the coroner. Typically, once a call is received from the hospital and the case is accepted by the MEC office, the charge nurse or other person calling should be asked the typical intake information (see Chapter 1). The DSI might need to go to the hospital to view the body or read the medical chart. The pathologist will want to read the chart before the autopsy, so copies are usually needed.

Reviewing Medical Records

The medical record is a large, voluminous collection of paper or electronic records that pertain to the care the patient received in the health-care facility. Some of this information is of little or no value in a death investigation. In other areas, such as the progress notes, the physician's writing is often illegible. The key to sorting through all this information is to know in which sections to look. One must keep in mind that summaries and other notes are dictated by the physician. These may take about 24 hours to type and put on the chart and might not be available when the chart is copied. This may necessitate going back to the hospital for information when it is typed. In any event, the *DSI should request the entire chart* because one does not know what part of the chart will be helpful to the investigation. The most important information can usually be obtained from the following sections of the hospital chart:

- *Discharge summary:* This is a summary of the chief complaint of the patient (the main reason the patient came to the hospital), the diagnosis, and the treatment given. Also, a timeline is given of the ups and downs of the patient's progress during the hospitalization. Because it is dictated by the main treating physician, the discharge summary often contains the rationale behind the diagnosis and therapy for the patient. It will also describe the condition of the patient when discharged and the medications the patient was prescribed. If the patient dies in the hospital, the discharge summary (sometimes called the death summary) may not have been typed before the information is needed. If not available, the main treating physician should be contacted, or the summary should be obtained, when typed.

- *History and physical:* This is the record of the admitting physician's examination, diagnosis, and plan for treatment. This document contains information the patient might have told the doctor on admission.
- *Consultation notes:* This is a record, similar to a history and physical, made by a specialist, such as a surgeon, after admission. These documents contain additional information about a particular patient problem and treatment.
- *Operative notes:* This is a record made by a surgeon describing the type of surgery and exactly how it was performed. For example, the operative note would describe where gunshot wounds and bullets were located and how they were managed.
- *Physician's notes or progress notes:* These notes are brief, daily summaries of the progress of the patient written by the treating physicians. These notes are often, but not always, illegible. They include patient symptoms and problems, new lab and x-ray results, and response to treatment. The end of the note usually states a future plan for the care of the patient.
- *Nurse's notes:* These notes are completed by a nurse during his or her shift, with notations being made several times during the shift. These notes are often the best indicator of how or what the patient was doing at a particular time of the day. Sudden changes in the patient's condition, such as the events around the time of death, are recorded. Often, the notes record the visitors present and how these visitors interact with the patient. Such notes might prove valuable when visitors later turn out to be suspect in the patient's death, as in child abuse cases where the parent might seem indifferent to the child's suffering.
- *Medication list:* This records show the drugs the patient has been given, along with the dosage and the times given. This list is useful to explain toxicology results.
- *Graphic record:* This contains the temperature, blood pressure, pulse, and respirations of the patient. Electronic records now often make this information part of the nurse's notes.

- *Laboratory results:* Lab results are a valuable part of the medical record and can be useful in explaining the cause of death. For example, a high white blood cell count can indicate infection, or an increased D-Dimer can indicate a pulmonary embolus (blood clot in the lung). Drug screen and alcohol results are found here as well.
- *Radiology (x-ray) or diagnostic imaging reports:* This is another valuable part of the record, containing everything from chest x-rays to computerized axial tomography (CAT) scans to magnetic resonance imaging (MRI) reports. These reports are useful to the autopsy pathologist in helping focus on problems, such as fractures, that were discovered during the hospitalization. If needed, copies of the actual image can easily be made because most film is stored digitally.
- *Social work notes:* This record is variable, depending on the patient and the availability of social services. These notes can be helpful in child or elder abuse cases where the social worker has interviewed family members and caretakers.

Medical records are important in natural and unnatural deaths. Hospital medical records should be obtained in all death investigations where the decedent died in or had even recently been in the hospital. Records from doctors' offices are more problem oriented. These records will contain correspondence from other specialists and some hospital records. These offices might not be inclined to give all information the first time asked. If the DSI finds information absent, a second request might be necessary.

Natural Diseases and Death Investigation   6

Introduction

More than half of all deaths investigated by a medical examiner/coroner's (MEC) office involve natural diseases, the most common being cardiovascular disease. Natural disease processes alter the way the body reacts to and repairs from injuries. The older the person, the more likely that natural disease has a role in the death. This concept can work in reverse. One can erroneously assume that because the person is young, natural disease is not a factor in the death. People with medical problems are frequently taking prescription medication, and these medications can have a bearing on the cause and manner of death. Many people have unknown or undiagnosed natural diseases that manifest in sudden, unexpected death. A common history in these cases is that "he hadn't seen a doctor in years" or "he didn't believe in doctors." In the author's experience, the result is that the first doctor he sees is the pathologist, who diagnoses what was a treatable natural disease such as cardiovascular disease. For these reasons, it is useful for all death scene investigators (DSIs) to become familiar with common medical diseases and conditions, as well as the associated terminology.

Sudden Death

"Sudden death" is a term used frequently in death investigation but its meaning can be ambiguous. In some situations, death can literally be *instantaneous*, such as with a massive pulmonary embolus. In others, such as a myocardial infarction, the death can be instantaneous, or take minutes to hours or longer. *Sudden cardiac death* is a sudden, unexpected death from cardiac causes within 1 hour of onset of symptoms (Cotran, R.S., Kumar V., and Collins, T.,

2003)). In some cases, the person is found and resuscitated, supported by ventilators and medical care, only to be declared brain dead days later. Some use the modifier "near" when describing this situation, such as "near SIDS (sudden infant death syndrome)" or "near drowning." In all these examples, the death is sudden and unexpected (not necessarily instantaneous), but the actual time between the onset of symptoms and the death can vary widely. Some authors consider "true" sudden death as instantaneous death, occurring within seconds of the onset of symptoms (DiMaio, V.J.M. and Dana, S.E., 2006.).

In some death investigations, the issue of survival time can become important. This is true in cases where actions were carried out by some person at the crime scene, and if the deceased were instantaneously dead, then another person must have carried out those actions. Depending on the disease or injury, and the actions taken, the pathologist can give an estimate as to whether those actions were possible. For example, a television was carried about 50 feet and dropped. If the person is found to have a massive pulmonary embolus, or gunshot wound of the brainstem, moving a television 50 feet is unlikely. However, one must be careful in these estimates because the author has seen a situation where a person was stabbed in the heart and did carry a television 50 feet.

Cardiac System

Ischemic Heart Disease (Atherosclerotic Cardiovascular Disease)

Ischemic heart disease (IHD) generally refers to a group of afflictions related to the decrease in or blockage of blood flow in the coronary arteries, the arteries that supply blood to the heart. "Ischemic" refers to the lack of oxygen and other nutrients that the blockage prevents the heart muscle from receiving. In the majority of cases, ischemia is due to atherosclerosis of the coronary arteries. Atherosclerosis is a type of arteriosclerosis where yellowish "plaque" builds up over time, eventually narrowing the lumen (center) of the artery and shutting off the blood supply. Also, this plaque and a weak blood vessel wall can balloon out (aneurysm) or rupture, further shutting off the blood flow. In less than 15% of cases, a blood clot (thrombus) can occlude the lumen as well (Cotran, R.S., Kumar V., and Collins, T., 2003).

IHD is responsible for 500,000 deaths each year (Cotran, R.S., Kumar V., and Collins, T., 2003.), and is the leading cause of natural death in men aged 20–65 years (DiMaio, V.J.M. and Dana, S.E., 2006). Risk factors include family history of heart disease, advancing age, high cholesterol, diabetes, smoking, and high blood pressure. IHD results in four different serious or potentially fatal conditions:

1. Myocardial infarction (heart attack)
2. Chronic IHD with heart failure (congestive heart failure or CHF)
3. Sudden cardiac death
4. Angina pectoris (chest pain)

Myocardial infarction is the result of decreased blood flow to the heart muscle, causing death of the muscle. This decreased blood flow can be due to a sudden blockage of the coronary artery as the result of a blood clot or dislodged plaque, for example. Also, when significant atherosclerotic blockage is present, the victim can put demand on the circulation by shoveling snow, for example, also causing an infarction. If the decrease in circulation is large enough or is in critical areas of the heart, death can occur within seconds to minutes (sudden cardiac death). These victims often have a fatal cardiac arrhythmia (heart block, ventricular fibrillation, tachycardia, bradycardia, etc.). At autopsy, the heart muscle will look grossly and microscopically normal, as no infarction will be seen. In fact, if the victim lives 4 hours after the infarction, only the earliest changes, "wavy fibers," will be seen under the microscope. Only if the victim lives longer than about 8 to 12 hours can the infarction be seen as mottling of the damaged muscle (Figure 6.1). After approximately 4 to 5 days, the dead muscle is very weak and at risk for rupture, causing a hemopericardium (Figure 6.2). The injury can heal, and after about 2 months leaves a characteristic whitish scar in the same area.

Figure 6.1 Acute myocardial infarction. This myocardial section shows mottling in the lateral left ventricular wall, suggesting early myocardial infarction. Infarction will be confirmed by examining tissue sections with the microscope. Marked mottling can be seen at the bottom of the figure, which is the anterior left ventricular wall.

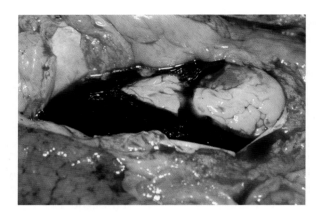

Figure 6.2 Hemopericardium. Blood clot can be seen filling the pericardium. This patient had suffered a myocardial infarction about 5 days previously. The infarcted (dead) heart tissue burst open, allowing for hemopericardium. The blood in the pericardium interferes with the contraction of the heart (cardiac *tamponade*), and can cause cardiac arrest.

Chronic IHD occurs over a long period of time. These victims suffer gradual ischemic damage due to slowly clogging arteries. There may be a history of healed infarction, previous cardiac bypass history, or no history at all. In addition to angina, these patients may have a history of shortness of breath and ankle edema, the latter of which often requires a diuretic (water pill), such as Lasix®. These patients can die suddenly due to arrhythmias, acute heart failure, pulmonary edema, and myocardial infarction, among other conditions.

Sudden cardiac death affects 300,000 to 400,000 persons per year and is generally defined as the sudden unexpected death, related to cardiac causes, occurring 1 hour or less from the onset of symptoms (Cotran, R.S., Kumar V., and Collins, T., 2003). Common causes related to sudden cardiac death include:

- Idiopathic (no cause is found)
- Ischemic heart disease
- Myocarditis (inflammation of the heart)
- Congenital heart disease
- Hypertensive heart disease (thick left ventricle and high blood pressure)
- Mitral valve prolapse ("floppy" heart valve)
- Aortic or subaortic stenosis
- Hereditary syndromes, such as the long QT syndrome

In myocarditis, the pathologist examines the heart muscle under the microscope to look for inflammation and death (necrosis) of cardiac muscle cells. In sudden cardiac deaths, the conduction system can be examined microscopically by the pathologist to demonstrate inflammation or scarring. Because the conduction system is the "electrical system" of the heart, interruption can cause arrhythmias. The autopsy itself cannot prove arrhythmia, but finding an interruption of the conduction system can be strong evidence for a fatal arrhythmia. In some cases, the heart is grossly and microscopically normal, but the circumstances of the death appear to be cardiac in origin (angina or chest pain, shortness of breath, sudden collapse, and the like). The autopsy may only show pulmonary edema and congestion. These victims likely suffer a fatal arrhythmia, and the heart defect that caused the arrhythmia is simply not detectable by the autopsy.

Angina Pectoris (chest pain) is a symptom of serious cardiac disease. Most patients have severe ischemic heart disease for which chest pain is a warning sign. Classically, the victim may have pain below the sternum (breast bone), often described as a crushing pain. The pain can radiate into the arms (usually the left), neck, jaws, and back. Evaluation of the cause of the chest pain can be difficult for the physician since many other conditions such as stomach ulcers, esophageal reflux, pulmonary emboli, and arthritis in the ribs can mimic chest pain of cardiac origin. Patients who have seen a physician and have been diagnosed with chest pain of cardiac origin might be prescribed cardiac drugs such as nitroglycerin. Diagnostic tests to evaluate this symptom include electrocardiogram (EKG), treadmill with an Adenosine stress test, Myoview scan, MUGA scan (Technetium nuclear scan for cardiac function), Echocardiogram and cardiac catheterization with or without angioplasty (to evaluate and open plaque blockages in the coronary arteries). Significant coronary atherosclerosis might require coronary artery bypass graft surgery in which the patient's own blood vessels are grafted to the aorta and coronary arteries to "bypass" the blocked arteries.

Respiratory System

Upper Respiratory System

Epiglottitis and "Café Coronary"

The trachea connects the mouth and nose to the lungs, normally allowing the free exchange of air. Air must travel through the pharynx and larynx (voice box) as it travels down to the lungs. The epiglottis is a thumb-shaped flap that closes when one swallows so that food cannot go into the trachea and lungs. In acute epiglottitis, bacterial inflammation of the epiglottis can cause severe swelling, cutting off the air flow and causing death (Figure 6.3a,b). A severe allergic reaction can cause swelling of the epiglottis and other tissues in the throat, also resulting in death. Food and foreign objects (usually in children) can be caught here as well. In adults who are either under the influence of central nervous system depressants such as alcohol, or are debilitated, the risk of choking is

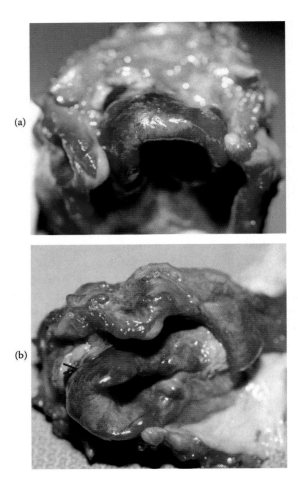

Figure 6.3 Epiglottitis. (a) Edema and swelling of the epiglottis can cause occlusion of the airway and death. (b) The rounded, meaty-red, swollen epiglottis shown here was the result of group B *Streptococcus* infection. The victim died suddenly with "trouble breathing" after having a severe sore throat for several days.

increased. A "café coronary" occurs when a person chokes on food while eating in a restaurant. A choking person cannot talk and may panic by getting up and running to the restroom, thus giving the appearance of a "coronary."

Lower Respiratory System

Pneumothorax

Pneumothorax simply means air in the chest (thoracic) cavity. If air leaks out of the lung, either spontaneously or by trauma, air goes into the thoracic cavity and the lung collapses. In patients with poor pulmonary function, or when severe or bilateral, if untreated, pneumothorax may result in death. A chest tube removes the air and allows the lung to reinflate.

Pulmonary Thromboembolus (PE) A thrombus is a blood clot. An embolus is anything moving through the vascular system, such as an air bubble, bullet, or a blood clot. Most pulmonary thromboemboli are formed in the deep veins of the calf muscles of the legs. Once the clot forms, it can move up through the larger veins into the right side of the heart, where it then moves into the pulmonary arteries (Figure 6.4). If the clot is large enough, it can cause acute right heart failure and instantaneous death. Smaller clots might only block a smaller artery and cause a pulmonary infarct, sending a warning that a larger clot may follow. These patients have shortness of breath and chest pain. There can be a history of leg swelling, redness, and pain. Conditions that pose a risk for PE include:

- Postoperative, especially orthopedic and fracture cases
- Cancer
- Trauma
- Elderly, bedridden, and debilitated
- Family history
- Previous history
- Burns
- Myocardial infarction and atrial fibrillation
- Genetic disorders (e.g., Factor V Leiden gene)

Asthma Asthma is a chronic inflammatory condition of the lungs in which the airways constrict (bronchospasm) and reduce air flow in the

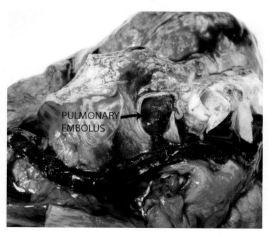

Figure 6.4 Pulmonary embolus (PE). Blood clots, usually from the lower extremities, can travel up the venous system to the right side of the heart, occluding the pulmonary arterial system. A clot this size can cause nearly instantaneous death.

lungs. Symptoms include wheezing, shortness of breath, and coughing. Sudden death is a risk in a small percentage (less than 5%) of cases (DiMaio, V.J.M. and Dana, S.E., 2006). Status asthmaticus is a sudden, severe asthma attack that can be fatal. If untreated, the lungs in status asthmaticus can appear overinflated at autopsy (Figure 6.5). Asthma patients usually have a long history of treatment, and the family is usually aware of the seriousness of the disease. Asthma "attacks" can be caused by many different triggers, including allergies, drugs, stress, exercise, industrial toxins (e.g., red cedar dust in lumbering), and unknown causes.

Pneumonia   Pneumonia is a general term for inflammation of the lung. The source of the inflammation can be bacterial, viral, fungal, or chemical. The inflammatory process reduces the air exchange capacity of the lungs (Figure 6.6). Most patients who acquire pneumonia in the community seek treatment, making the number of fatal cases low. However, untreated fatal cases of pneumonia are often found in alcoholics, drug addicts, debilitated and chronically ill patients, and those individuals with a weak immune system (immunosuppressed). Pneumonia is often a complication in many situations seen by the MEC. These include nearly any patient on a respiratory ventilator for a prolonged period of time, massive trauma, and burns. Patients who aspirate develop a chemical pneumonia from the gastric acid irritating the lung tissue, and then bacteria invade secondarily, causing further inflammation. Industrial exposure to certain compounds (e.g., chlorine gas) can also cause chemical pneumonia.

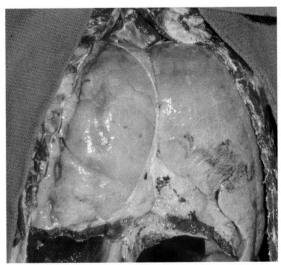

Figure 6.5 Hyperinflated, asthmatic lungs. The lungs here show hyperinflation due to trapping of air. This patient died of a sudden asthma attack (*status asthmaticus*), where bronchial spasm and plugging of mucus hamper breathing, causing air to be trapped.

Figure 6.6 Purulent material in the smaller bronchus. On further sectioning, this lung shows yellowish, mucoid pus in the bronchi, indicating bronchopneumonia.

Massive, Fatal Hemoptysis Hemoptysis is coughing or "spitting up" blood. Individuals with cancer of the lung or respiratory tree, tuberculosis (TB), lung abscess, or aortic aneurysm eroding into the lung can experience a sudden, fatal hemoptysis. A common scene finding is abundant blood in the bathroom. Ruptured esophageal varices, a complication of cirrhosis of the liver, should be ruled out.

Emphysema and Chronic Bronchitis: Chronic Obstructive Pulmonary Disease (COPD) The majority of these diseases are caused by cigarette smoking; approximately 10% of patients are nonsmokers (Cotran, R.S., Kumar V., and Collins, T., 2003). Emphysema and chronic bronchitis are both classified as COPD. The lung tissue is damaged to the point where the air exchanging ability of the lung is gradually reduced and the air sacs dilate, trapping air. In later stages, these patients require continuous oxygen. If the oxygen is removed, or the tank is empty, death can ensue. These patients are very vulnerable to dying from pneumonia. The inflammation hinders the air exchange ability of the small amount of lung tissue remaining.

Pulmonary Edema and Congestion Congestion in the lungs is accumulation of blood in the vascular system. This is commonly due to the blood being "backed up" in the lungs, not being moved out by the heart. Soon, pulmonary edema can occur as fluid or even blood leaks out into the air spaces (alveoli) (Figure 6.7a, b). The patient becomes short of breath and can ominously cough up a white, pink, or red foamy fluid. The air exchange ability of the lung is further compromised, which eventually makes the edema worse. Pulmonary edema is the end result of many different problems in the body. The problems include:

- Myocardial infarction and heart failure
- Drug overdose

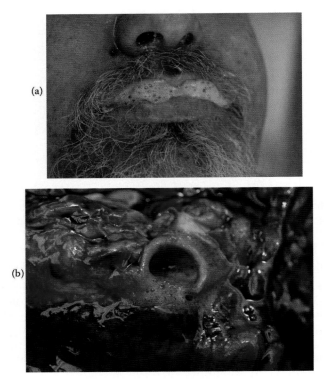

(a)

(b)

Figure 6.7 Pulmonary edema. (a) Pink-to-red fluid exuding from the mouth and nose indicates severe pulmonary edema. This fluid can be propelled upward from the lungs after death, especially if the body falls in a position where gravity allows it to flow out. (b) Centrally in the bronchus, the lung section shows edema fluid characterized by fluid exuding from the air-filled spaces, producing bubbles. Common causes of pulmonary edema include heart failure, drug overdoses, and central nervous system pathology. Fluid engorges the vascular system, causing fluid to exude into the air spaces, mixing with air, forming a foamy, bloody fluid.

- Shock
- Trauma
- Brain injury
- Brain hemorrhage and strokes
- Pneumonia and sepsis
- Any death where the heart slowly fails

Acute respiratory distress syndrome (ARDS) or "shock lung" is a condition in which the lung capillaries are damaged, severely interfering with air exchange. This condition can be seen after shock, trauma, and sepsis.

Gastrointestinal Tract and Pancreas

Massive, Fatal Hematemesis (Vomiting Blood)

Hematemesis can come from the stomach or esophagus. Blood from the stomach can be dark and coffee-grounds appearing. Cirrhosis patients develop varices in the esophagus, which are dilated veins. Because cirrhosis renders the liver hard, blood backs up into the veins of the esophagus that connect to the liver. These veins can rupture spontaneously, causing death in 40% to 50% of cases (Cotran, R.S., Kumar V., and Collins, T., 2003). Mallory-Weiss tears can cause severe bleeding. Severe vomiting and retching can cause a tear where the esophagus inserts into the stomach.

Ulcers and cancers of the stomach can erode into a large blood vessel and cause severe bleeding as well. Stomach ulcers can also perforate the stomach wall, allowing gastric juices to flow into the abdominal cavity, causing a severe infection (peritonitis), and at times, death (Figure 6.8).

Bowel Infarctions

If a portion of the small or large bowel dies, bacteria can invade the abdominal cavity and cause peritonitis with later sepsis and shock (Figure 6.9). Bowel infarction can be caused by atherosclerosis of bowel arteries, thrombosis, hernias (incarcerated), twisted bowel (volvulus), tumors, and adhesions (scars from old inflammation or surgery).

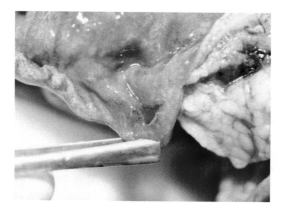

Figure 6.8 Perforated gastric ulcer. Central, above the forceps is a hole that goes completely through the stomach. Once the stomach perforates, the situation is life threatening as the patient needs immediate surgery. Perforation causes a near immediate chemical (due to stomach acids) and bacterial peritonitis, leading to infection and death unless immediate medical attention is sought.

Figure 6.9 Bowel infarction. Bowel infarction will cause shock, peritonitis, and death if not treated immediately by surgery. Bacteria from the dead bowel seep into the peritoneum, where it can easily spread throughout the body, causing shock and death.

Pancreatitis

The pancreas contains many enzymes that aid in digesting food normally. If the pancreas becomes inflamed, these enzymes can be released into the abdominal cavity and the surrounding tissues can be digested. Pancreatitis is a serious condition that can lead to pancreatic hemorrhage, low serum calcium, sepsis, shock, and death. Pancreatitis can be seen in alcoholism, trauma, and with stones blocking the drainage of the pancreatic ducts.

Liver

Fatty Change or Fatty Metamorphosis

A number of conditions and toxins can cause fat to accumulate in the liver cells, giving the liver a yellowish gross appearance (Figure 6.10). While some cases of severe fatty liver are associated with sudden death, most cases are not fatal. Fatty liver is associated with many conditions and diseases as listed below, including:

- Alcohol abuse
- Diabetes
- Hepatitis
- Starvation
- Obesity
- Many drugs and toxins (e.g., tetracycline)

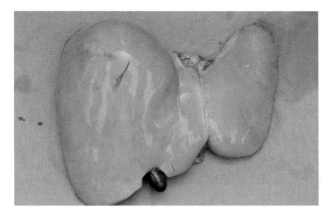

Figure 6.10 Fatty liver. Fatty liver can be seen in many conditions (see text). When the liver is acutely damaged by drugs, toxins, or diseases, the response is for the cells to become fatty. The degree of fatty change is determined under the microscope.

Cirrhosis

Cirrhosis is a response of the liver to damage over a period of time (Figure 6.11). Alcoholism is the cause most people think of as causing cirrhosis. Only about 10% to 15% of alcoholics develop cirrhosis (Cotran, R.S., Kumar V., and Collins, T., 2003). Hepatitis B and C (not hepatitis A), hemachromatosis (iron overload), and other conditions can also lead to cirrhosis. Some of these patients are eligible and can receive liver transplants.

In alcoholism, the development of cirrhosis seems to primarily depend on the amount of alcohol consumed and the inherited decrease in specific enzymes that protect the liver. Because some major clotting factors are made in the liver, in the later stages of cirrhosis, these patients are prone to bleeding. The liver can fail outright, causing fatal metabolic problems in the body (e.g., elevated ammonia levels). Formation of varices in the esophagus, which are prone to bleeding, is another complication. Cirrhosis is associated with sudden death, as is alcoholism.

Hepatitis

Hepatitis simply means inflammation of the liver. Normally, hepatitis refers to viral hepatitis, which includes hepatitis A, B, C, D, E, and G. Hepatitis A is acquired by ingesting virus-contaminated food or water. Although highly contagious, it is transmitted by contaminated feces, not blood. Hepatitis A does not cause chronic hepatitis or cirrhosis.

Figure 6.11 Cirrhosis of the liver. The sections of liver shown are very hard. Cirrhosis is simply a scarring of the liver. It is the way the liver reacts to an injury over a period of time. The injury can be alcohol, an acetaminophen overdose, or chronic ischemia due to heart failure. In cirrhosis, the liver becomes very hard, so that blood cannot flow normally through the liver. This causes the blood to back up elsewhere in the body, such as the esophagus (esophageal varices). Also, the liver begins to fail due to a lack of cells to do the work, like making clotting factors. As a result, the patient is prone to spontaneous bleeding. A common problem is for a cirrhotic patient to rupture the dilated veins around the esophagus, and clotting is less likely to occur. When advanced, this condition is irreversible and very commonly fatal.

Hepatitis B, C, D, and G are all contracted by a blood-borne route, and less commonly through sexual intercourse. Hepatitis B, C, and D can cause chronic hepatitis, with hepatitis C being the most likely. Cirrhosis and hepatocellular carcinoma are later complications.

The DSI and everyone involved in handling the body and body fluids should treat every case as infectious, using universal precautions. While it is prudent to warn everyone involved in handling the body and bodily fluids that the deceased is known to have hepatitis, one should keep in mind that it the unknown case that is the most dangerous.

Vascular System

Aortic Aneurysm and Aortic Dissection

An aneurysm of the aorta is a ballooning of the wall. The wall can become weak due to atherosclerosis or elastic defects in the wall (Figure 6.12). At some point, the aneurysm can rupture, causing massive hemorrhage. Depending on the location, the blood can dissect into the pericardium, chest cavity, and abdominal cavity.

An aortic dissection is a simple dissection of blood through a weakness in the aortic wall. As with an aneurysm, massive fatal hemorrhage can occur.

Figure 6.12 Abdominal aortic aneurysm. The aneurysm is cut open to reveal a thick, layered aneurysm wall. The finger is pointing at this wall. Focal hemorrhage into the wall can be seen below. Aneurysms that rupture during life cause massive internal bleeding and are often fatal unless prompt, emergent vascular surgery is performed.

Central Nervous System (CNS) Disorders

Epilepsy (Seizure Disorder)

The history of seizure disorder warrants some investigation. Patients with generalized seizures (jerking movements of the entire body with loss of consciousness) are usually on medications, such as Dilantin® or Tegretol®, to decrease the frequency of seizures. If the patient stops taking the medication for some reason, the seizures can become more frequent. Prolonged seizures (*status epilepticus*) can be fatal, as effective breathing does not occur. Epileptics are at risk for sudden death but the mechanism of death can be a seizure or a cardiac arrhythmia in some cases. If alcoholics suddenly stop drinking, seizure-like activity (alcohol-withdrawal seizures) can result, which can also be fatal. For this reason, some alcoholics are given seizure medications.

At autopsy, the findings usually only include pulmonary edema and contusion of tongue. Occasionally, the seizure victim will display "instant rigor mortis," with body parts recapitulating the spasm of the seizure (Figure 6.13). The brain usually does not show an abnormality but when it does, a tumor, vascular malformation, or an old injury is seen (post-traumatic seizure disorder).

Subarachnoid Hemorrhage

Subarachnoid hemorrhage in the absence of trauma is usually due to a ruptured berry (saccular) aneurysm or arteriovenous malformation (AVM). The subarachnoid layer of the brain is the one tightly fitted around the outside

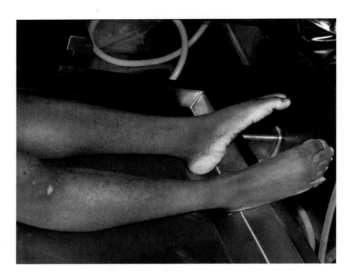

Figure 6.13 Pedal spasms in a seizure death. Generalized seizures (grand mal) cause violent convulsions. If these convulsions are prolonged, the victim cannot breathe effectively, and death ensues. In this case, rigor occurred quickly due to the intense muscular activity of the seizure, showing the spasms of the foot.

of the brain so that when the brain is removed, the blood is kept close to the brain by this tightly fitting layer. The aneurysm is on the bottom of the brain, in a collection of arteries called the "circle of Willis" (Figure 6.14). Some 80% of people die within 24 hours of rupture. Some patients experience the rupture while performing some rigorous physical activity such as sexual intercourse or lifting objects.

Strokes

Strokes can either be hemorrhagic or ischemic. In both cases, there is significant damage to brain tissue. This damage can cause death by brain swelling, hemorrhage, and direct damage to vital centers of the brain. Causes of hemorrhagic stroke include hypertension, AVM, anticoagulant overdose, and tumors (Figure 6.15). Causes of an ischemic stroke include atherosclerosis and other blockage of arteries, venous thrombosis, and global ischemia from lack of blood flow in all areas, such as in a cardiac arrest patient.

Meningitis

Meningitis is the inflammation of the meninges, the layers that cover the brain and spinal cord. The most common cause is bacterial, although viruses and fungi can cause meningitis as well. The meninges appear cloudy, and occasionally pus can be seen. The cerebral spinal fluid should be cultured

Figure 6.14 Ruptured berry (saccular) aneurysm. An aneurysmal blood vessel at the base of the brain can rupture spontaneously, causing subarachnoid hemorrhage. Blood appears at the base of the brain. The offending blood vessel was removed here, showing ballooning between the 2- and 3-cm marks, and a normal size between the 3- and 4-cm marks.

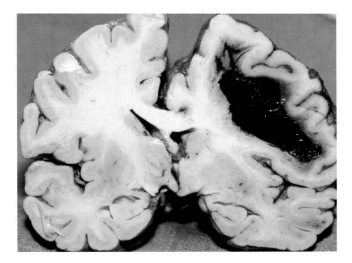

Figure 6.15 Intracerebral hemorrhage. This section of brain shows hemorrhage in the white matter. This patient had a history of hypertension.

if meningitis is suspected, so that those in contact with the deceased can be given prophylactic treatment. Common bacteria causing meningitis include *Neisseria meningitidis* (meningococcus) and *Streptococcus pneumoniae*. Meningococcus can present in young adults who live close together, such as military recruits and college students. A vaccine is available, however. These patients present with headache, neck pain, and fever.

Encephalitis

Encephalitis is inflammation of the brain, usually caused by viruses. Recently, an epidemic of West Nile viral encephalitis broke out in the Midwest. Other types of encephalitis in the United States include Eastern and Western Equine, Venezuelan, St. Louis, and La Crosse. These patients present with headache, sleepiness, seizures, confusion, and coma. These cases are important to identify for public health reasons.

Systemic Diseases

Carcinomatosis

The term "cancer" refers to an abnormal growth of cells in the body that have the capacity to grow and spread throughout the body (metastasize). "Malignant" refers to the behavior of the cancer to cause significant illness and/or death. Cancer is not simply one disease. Virtually every organ and tissue in the body has a malignant counterpart that can cause severe health problems, including death, by local or distant spread. Each type of malignancy behaves differently in the body. The same cancer in two different people can even behave differently. In most malignancies, the patient gets an extensive diagnostic workup including surgery with resection or biopsy of the tumor, x-rays, and scans. After the malignancy is classified and the extent of spread of the tumor is determined, treatment can begin.

Cancer patients can appear to be doing well and free of disease (remission), and then suddenly fall ill again (relapse). This phenomenon can be difficult for families, especially when the person dies suddenly after a relapse. The families may blame the care or other factors for the death and demand an autopsy. The DSI should research the medical records and the situation, but most cases can be signed out without an autopsy.

Cancer patients can die suddenly for several reasons, including:

- Erosion or impingement of the tumor on adjacent structures: a lung cancer can erode into an artery causing hemorrhage.
- Production of by-products that harm the body: tumors can cause the body to produce calcium or form blood clots.
- Secondary infections: cancer patients are very susceptible to sepsis, pneumonia, and other infections.
- Cancer cachexia: it is well known that cancer patients "waste away" and have poor appetites. The patient loses weight and has muscle wastage to the point where death can occur.
- Carcinomatosis: cancer patients, particularly those with widely spread malignancies, can die suddenly with no additional apparent mechanism of death (Figure 6.16).

Sepsis, Shock, and Death

Sepsis is a generalized bacterial infection in the blood. It is a serious, life-threatening infection that must be treated immediately. The bacteria can quickly cause vascular collapse in the body (shock) and disseminated intravascular coagulation (DIC). Certain bacteria, most notoriously Gram-negative bacteria, can more rapidly cause these problems. DIC is a process where the bacteria cause most of the clotting factors to be activated throughout the

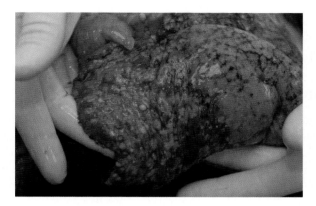

Figure 6.16 Carcinomatosis displayed in the lung. Multiple white metastatic nodules can be seen, particularly in the left side of the figure. Patients with disseminated or widely metastatic carcinoma can die suddenly for no readily apparent physiologic reason. "Metastatic Carcinoma" or "Carcinomatosis" are acceptable causes of death in such cases.

body, consuming them. At this point, with most of the factors consumed, the patient begins to bleed uncontrollably. There is no good treatment for DIC, except supporting the patient, administering blood products, and treating the infection that caused it.

Diabetes Mellitus

The hallmark of diabetes mellitus is elevated blood glucose due to the lack of insulin production by the pancreas. There are two types of diabetes, namely types I and II. Type I is a more severe form that usually starts in childhood and becomes more severe with age. Type I can develop at any age. The patients are more "brittle," showing greater variation in glucose levels and requiring more insulin. Both types show genetic factors.

Type II diabetes is sometimes referred to as "adult onset diabetes." Obesity, poor diet, and lack of physical activity are strong factors in the development of this disease later in life. These patients can often reduce their insulin requirements by losing weight and modifying their diets.

There are many long- and short-term serious complications of diabetes. If the patient does not take insulin, the blood glucose can increase to 600 mg/dL or greater over a short period of time, potentially causing a diabetic coma, which is life threatening. Also, if too much insulin is given, the glucose can drop to below 40 mg/dL, causing unconsciousness and death unless glucose can be given immediately. The long-term, potentially lethal complications of diabetes include:

- High blood pressure
- Stroke

- Coronary atherosclerosis and myocardial infarction
- Systemic atherosclerosis, involving aorta and leg arteries
- Kidney disease leading to renal failure

Alcohol Abuse

Alcohol (ethanol) abuse is responsible for at least 100,000 deaths per year in the United States, and ethanol is the most commonly abused drug worldwide (Cotran, R.S., Kumar V., and Collins, T., 2003). Anyone who has worked in law enforcement, medicine, or death investigation is well aware of the effects of alcohol on human behavior.

Initially, alcohol produces euphoria or exhilaration, followed by loss of inhibition, talkativeness, slurred speech, unsteady gait and other balance and coordination problems, drowsiness, stupor, and finally coma. Ultimately, ethanol is a depressant leading to a wide variety of behaviors, including suicide and homicide.

A blood level of 0.08 g/dL is the legal limit for driving in most states, although impairment begins as low as 0.03 g/dL. To reach 0.08 g/dL in a 175-pound person requires about four 12-ounce beers, four 1.5-ounce, 90-proof spirit drinks, or four 6-ounce glasses of wine. Drowsiness and stupor can occur at 0.2 g/dL or less in nondrinkers, and death can occur at 0.25 g/dL or greater. Alcoholics can tolerate very high levels, even drive, walk, and perform other tasks at 0.50 g/dL or greater. Postmortem levels of ethanol might not reflect the highest level the individual attained after drinking, because the person might have lived in a coma for a period of time, metabolizing the ethanol.

Toxicology labs measure blood ethanol, but hospital labs measure serum alcohol. This can create some confusion because the two results are not interchangeable. Generally, serum levels are 1.18 times the blood levels, or 18% higher. Therefore, a *serum* alcohol level of 0.118 g/dL (118 mg/dL or 118 mg %) corresponds to a *blood* level of 0.100 g/dL.

Alcohol abuse and alcoholism affect many organs and tissues. Some of the effects are reversible while others are not. These effects include:

- Nervous system: unsteady gait and memory loss.
- Liver: fatty change and cirrhosis.
- Pancreas: acute and chronic pancreatitis.
- Heart: atrial fibrillation and cardiomyopathy.
- Stomach: gastritis.
- Skeletal muscle: weakness and pain.
- Testes: atrophy.
- Reproductive: fetal alcohol syndrome (birth defect).
- Metabolic: magnesium and thiamine deficiencies.

Human Immunodeficiency Virus (HIV)/Acquired Immune Deficiency Syndrome (AIDS)

HIV is a virus that attacks the white blood cells, causing an immune deficiency and leaving the body susceptible to opportunistic infections and cancers. AIDS is the name of this syndrome. By the end of 2002, nearly 900,000 cases were reported in the United States, and AIDS was the second most common cause of death in individuals between 25 and 44 (Cotran, R.S., Kumar V., and Collins, T., 2003). HIV is most commonly transmitted by sexual intercourse, both heterosexual and homosexual. Intravenous drug users sharing needles is another mode of infection. HIV can be acquired by needle sticks or other exposures to body fluids. Fortunately, cases of persons contacting HIV from a deceased person are very rare. Using universal precautions will prevent transmission of HIV.

The primary problem with HIV infection is the loss of a white blood cell called the CD4+ helper-inducer T cell. This allows normally harmless bacteria, protozoa, and other organisms to infect the body. Also, the patient is susceptible to certain cancers, such as lymphoma. Most HIV patients are well known in the medical community, and the deaths do not come into the medical examiner's jurisdiction unless there is a homicide or other unnatural death.

Traumatic Injuries

7

Blunt Force Injuries versus Sharp Force Injuries

The Importance of Terminology

Forensic pathologists commonly distinguish blunt force and sharp force injuries when describing wounds. When describing these wounds, the words used to describe injuries such as contusion, laceration, abrasion, stab wound, incised wound, etc., carry great weight because they have a specific meaning and context. Precise description and meaning of wounds is important for several reasons. Describing a wound as a laceration tells the investigator to look for a blunt object, rather than a knife or other sharp object. Common definitions for wounds allow for communication between investigators. In legal proceedings, it is important to use standard terminology and a reproducible description of findings.

Blunt Force Injuries

Blunt force injuries are visible changes of tissue caused by a scraping, hitting, crushing, shearing, tearing, or similar blunt force. The appearance and severity of the injury depends on the *amount* of force applied, the *object* used to transmit the force (e.g., narrow versus broad), the *part of the body injured* (bony area versus soft area), and the *condition* of the tissue injured (muscular and fit versus fragile and diseased). Blunt force injures can be sustained if the object strikes the body, if the body strikes the object, or a combination of both. Blunt force injuries include:

- Contusions
- Abrasions
- Lacerations
- Fractures of bones

- Avulsions
- Crush injuries

Features of Blunt Force Injuries

These blunt force injuries often appear together. For example, lacerations are nearly always accompanied by abrasions. Crush injuries may show all types of blunt force injury. Blunt force injuries often result in a loss of tissue that is transferred to the object causing the injury. This might be a small amount of tissue in a simple laceration or large amount of tissue in an avulsion injury. Objects will also transfer material to the wound (e.g., wood splinters from a board). All blunt force injuries should be examined for transferred material.

Contusions

A contusion, commonly known as a bruise, is a hemorrhage into skin or tissues caused by a blunt force that tears blood vessels. The leaking of blood discolors tissues, causing purplish-red or dark red discoloration. Since this is a visual process, certain factors alter what can be seen (Figure 7.1):

- Deep contusions might not be seen except at autopsy.
- Contusions are harder to see in people with a dark complexion.
- Elderly, malnourished, and ill individuals are more likely to bruise.
- Children may be more likely to bruise on the surface, but deep bruises may be difficult to see without an autopsy (Figure 7.2a,b).

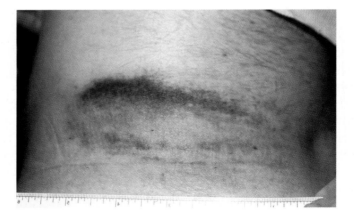

Figure 7.1 Contusion. This contusion is on a living person who was thrown into the wire rigging of a sailboat. The central clearing of the contusion is where the wire struck the skin. The blood is "milked" and forced from the central area of contact to the periphery. The contusion is about 4 days old (by history), and a golden brown hue can be seen in the center of the lesion (see text regarding healing contusions).

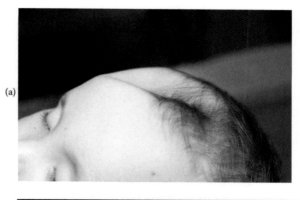

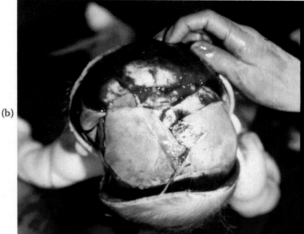

Figure 7.2 Depressed skull fracture with no visible contusion. (a) A depressed skull fracture can be seen clearly, but no contusion is visible. (b) When the scalp and galea is reflected back, extensive contusion hemorrhage can be seen. This illustrates the value of autopsies in children because contusions can be hidden.

- People with cirrhosis, liver failure, and bleeding disorders will bruise more easily, as do those on certain medications (e.g., Coumadin®).
- The site of hemorrhage does not always correlate with the injury because blood drains along the path of least resistance (e.g., "raccoon eyes" in a skull fracture (Figure 7.3).

Special types of hemorrhage into tissues include:

- *Hematomas:* literally "blood tumors," or large collections of blood in or around the tissue (Figure 7.4).
- *Ecchymoses:* large, confluent areas of hemorrhage under the skin (Figure 7.5; see also Figure 4.5).
- *Petechiae:* small, pinpoint or slightly larger, hemorrhages in a tissue (Figure 7.6).

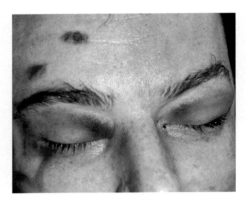

Figure 7.3 Orbital ecchymoses or "raccoon eyes." The darkening of the soft tissue around the eyes is due to blood accumulating in the soft tissues. This finding alerts the pathologist to search for fractures in the base of the skull, most likely the frontal bone or orbital roofs.

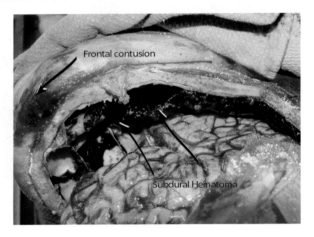

Figure 7.4 Subdural hematoma. A large hematoma can be seen between the brain and the dura, shown by the arrow. The pressure of the hematoma can affect the function of the brain, resulting in coma and death. This hematoma was produced by the deceased falling and striking his forehead. The small veins bridging the dura and the brain happened to be torn during the fall, resulting in hemorrhage.

Color Changes in Contusions

Generally, contusions change color after a period of time. Estimating the age of a contusion by the color is neither reliable nor predictable, and should only be given in general terms. Soon after it occurs, the contusion is red-purple or dark blue (minutes to hours). In the next few days, the color tends to be dark purple. After about a 5 to 7 days, the body then breaks down the hemoglobin in the tissue, turning the contusion green to dark yellow/brown, and then to pale yellow. Resolution can be from 10 days to a month or more (Figure 7.7). Occasionally, these changes will occur out of order. These changes are highly variable.

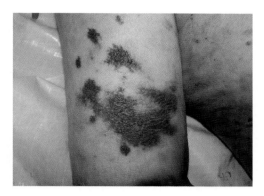

Figure 7.5 Ecchymoses (see Figure 4.5).

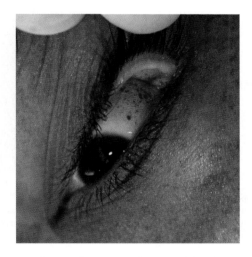

Figure 7.6 Conjunctival petechiae. Small point like hemorrhages in the conjunctiva, or clear membrane of the eye, are often seen in asphyxial deaths. These petechiae are due to hemorrhage of small vessels in the conjunctiva, caused by the increased vascular pressure seen in asphyxia.

Abrasions

An abrasion is the denuding of skin or tissue caused by a blunt or rough blunt object. An abrasion is also commonly known as a "scrape." There are four major types of abrasions:

1. *Abrasion (usual type):* due to an object contacting skin or tissue parallel to its surface (Figure 7.8).
2. *Sliding abrasion:* more linear and intense than a usual abrasion, it is caused when movement or sliding is involved. The abrasion lines show the direction of sliding (Figure 7.9).

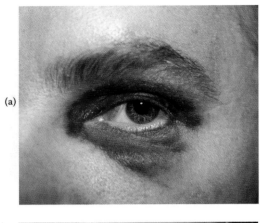

Figure 7.7 Healing contusions. Photograph was taken (a) 3 days after the author was struck in the orbit, and (b) 5 days after being struck. Note that the greenish rim around the central purple hemorrhage has began to turn golden brown or yellowish brown after only 2 days.

3. *Pressure abrasion:* when a heavy object or force compresses tissue in a mostly perpendicular direction (Figure 7.10).
4. *Pattern abrasion:* often the combination of several abrasion types forming a pattern reminiscent of the blunt object that contacted the skin (Figure 7.11).

Because abrasions involve the scraping away of skin, this skin can be transferred to the object causing the abrasion.

Lacerations (Tears)

A laceration is the tearing or splitting of skin caused by a blunt force object carrying force. Lacerations show at least three characteristics (Figure 7.12):

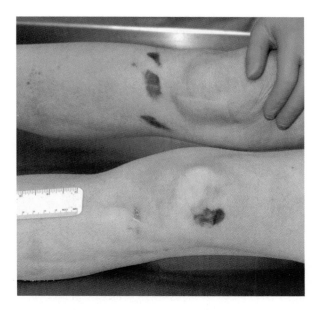

Figure 7.8 Usual abrasions. Abrasions are the pattern in the skin caused by a blunt object denuding the skin. This victim of a motor vehicle crash shows usual abrasions on the knees, commonly known as "scrapes."

1. Undermined and jagged margins
2. Tissue bridging
3. Abraded margins

Do not confuse a laceration with a cut!

Lacerations can be straight or jagged in shape. A common mistake is to call a straight laceration a cut (Figure 7.13). A cut is really an incised wound, which is a sharp force injury — that is, the tissue is cut, not torn. This is a very important distinction. The author recalls one case where the police were looking for a knife (because the laceration was straight) when the murder weapon was actually a baseball bat. Lacerations can be straight but will usually have undermined (and jagged) margins, tissue bridging, and abraded margins. The laceration in Figure 7.13 is classified as a laceration because it shows these three criteria — not because it is straight. The laceration is straight because the victim fell against the straight edge of a table during a seizure.

Configuration of Lacerations

The configuration of lacerations largely depends on the area of the body injured and the presence of underlying bony structures. Other important factors include the size, shape, surface, angle, and force of the object contacting the

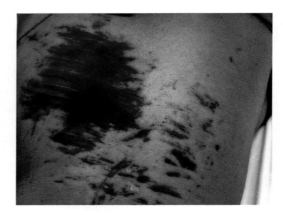

Figure 7.9 Sliding abrasion. This victim was thrown out of a moving vehicle. The long axis of the abrasions shows the direction in which the body moved across the pavement.

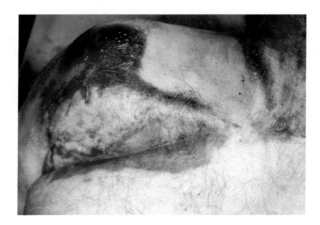

Figure 7.10 Pressure abrasion. The shoulder shows a yellow indentation below a purplish thermal burn. This victim's shoulder was wedged in a roller mechanism, whose shear force crushed the shoulder. The pressure flattened and thinned the skin so that the fat beneath shows through. The roller mechanism was also hot, producing the thermal burn on the upper part of the shoulder.

skin. The same object and force striking the soft, boneless region of the abdomen will cause a much different injury around the mouth area (Figure 7.14).

Avulsions

Avulsion is the tearing away of tissue. In an avulsion, tissue is hanging from, or completely missing from the body. The remaining margins show

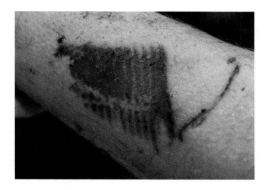

Figure 7.11 Patterned abrasion. This individual struck a solid object in his vehicle at a high rate of speed, causing this patterned abrasion of the leg. Automotive aficionados will recognize this as a General Motors type–brake pedal. Studying patterned abrasions can be useful in that they can leave an outline of the object that caused the injury.

Figure 7.12 Laceration of the scalp with marginal abrasion. Blunt force striking the skin with sufficient force tears the skin, resulting in tissue bridging, undermined margins, and a marginal abrasion.

laceration-like borders, except the tearing is often deep, involving bone, tendon, muscle, and other tissues (Figure 7.15). The scene should be searched for the avulsed tissue, and this tissue should be collected. If the tissue is found later, it could reflect badly on the MEC office. If the tissue cannot be found, one should think about where it might be, such as a second scene. Essentially, this missing tissue is evidence.

Figure 7.13 Laceration of the forehead. This laceration looks like a cut because it is straight. Careful observation, however, reveals tissue bridging, undermined margins, and marginal abrasion.

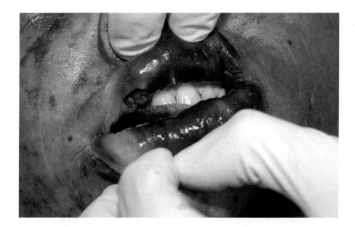

Figure 7.14 Laceration of the lip due to underlying teeth. The configuration of a laceration depends on underlying bony structures. In this figure, the lip was lacerated as it became sandwiched between the fist that caused the contusion and laceration and the teeth below. A similar blow to a soft area, like the stomach, would likely not have caused a laceration.

Crush Injuries

Crush injuries involve tremendous forces and large objects. The object(s) causing the injuries are usually not difficult to find due to the sheer size. Characteristics of crush injures include:

- Combination of all blunt force injuries
- Deep injuries to tissues such as laceration of organs
- Accidental deaths such as automobile crashes and industrial accidents
- Fracture of bones

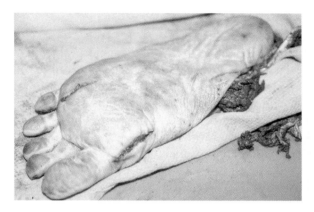

Figure 7.15 Avulsion of the foot. Airplane crashes impart tremendous force to tissues, causing shearing and shredding of the entire body. Intact body parts can be difficult to find in high-speed airplane crashes.

Fractures

Fractures of bones generally require a large amount of force. Exceptions include the elderly with osteoporosis, where fractures can even occur spontaneously with normal activity, such as walking. Children and young adults have pliable bones that bend, but do not break as easily. In the extremities and elsewhere, children tend to get greenstick fractures, where the bone bends like a young, green sapling. Bone fractures are caused by direct and indirect trauma (DiMaio, V.J.M. and Dana, S.E., 2006). *Direct fractures* are classified as follows:

- *Focal fracture:* a small to medium force striking a focal bone.
- *Crush fracture:* a large force over a large area, often breaking the bone into multiple pieces (comminution) and causing soft tissue injury.
- *Penetrating fracture:* an object striking bone with great force in a concentrated area (e.g., a bullet).

Indirect fractures are caused by a force acting outside or away from the bone. Types of indirect fractures include:

- *Rotational fracture:* the bone is twisted, causing a fracture, such as abusively twisting the arm or leg of a child.
- *Traction fracture:* the bone is literally pulled apart.
- *Angulation fracture:* the bone is traumatically bent at an angle until it snaps, leaving an angular fracture line.
- *Compression fracture:* the bone is compressed, causing fracture. In osteoporosis patients, the weight of the body can cause a vertebra to collapse or "compress."

Sharp Force Injuries

Sharp force injuries are generally made by a sharp object cutting the skin (except for special incised wounds, such as ice pick wounds), and commonly called a "cut." This is as opposed to a laceration, which is caused by tearing the skin. A common mistake is to call cuts "lacerations." This wrong classification of the wound can lead to the police looking for a baseball bat instead of a knife!

Types of sharp force injuries include:

- Incised wounds
- Stab wounds
- Puncture wounds
- Defense wounds or "cuts"
- Hesitation wounds, "marks," or "cuts"
- Chopping wounds

Stab Wounds

A stab wound is a cut of the skin or other tissue that is generally deeper than it is wide, caused by a sharp object like a knife, piece of glass, shiv, or similar object. Because stab wounds involve deep arteries, veins, and organs, the mechanism of death in these cases is often hemorrhage. The configuration of a knife stab wound depends on the sharpness of the blade. Most blades are sharp on one side and dull on the other, creating a V-shaped mark on the sharp end and a blunt or pyramid-shaped wound on the other end. (Figure 7.16).

Abrasions in and around the stab wound are caused by features on the knife. "Hilt marks" are caused by the handle and the attached (finger) guard. Other features such as serrations or other adornments on the knife can leave abrasions (Figure 7.17).

Unlike gunshot wounds where a bullet can be matched to a specific gun, knives can only rarely be matched to a specific wound. Cases where the perpetrator's fingerprints or the deceased's blood are on the knife allow matching to a specific knife. Also, if the knife, scissors, or other sharp instrument tip hits bone, it can break off and be matched up by tool marks to the purported sharp instrument (Figure 7.18a,b). Knife length and width cannot be reliably predicted by wound measurements. Tissue is very stretchable, so even a short blade can penetrate deeply. A long knife might not have been fully inserted. However, if multiple stab wounds are present, an experienced pathologist can give a range of possible knife lengths. Absent some specific information, such as DNA, the pathologist can usually only opine that the wound(s) is(are) consistent or not consistent with a purported knife.

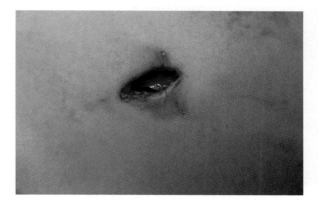

Figure 7.16 Stab wound. This wound displays a pointed end at the 9 o'clock portion of the wound. The other end of the wound shows a more blunted area. Small dots are seen at 12 o'clock and 4 o'clock where the wound was stitched together at the hospital. The sharp edge of the knife caused the 9 o'clock or sharp part of the wound, while the opposite end was caused by the blunt edge of the knife.

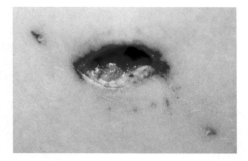

Figure 7.17 Stab wound with hilt mark. Stab wounds are deeper than they are long. This stab wound demonstrates that the full length of the knife was thrust into the body. The abrasion on the wound, and the radial marks surrounding the wound, were caused by the hilt, or end, of the knife. The two outside abrasions were caused by the finger guards of the knife. These characteristic marks could be used to exclude or include unknown knives in an investigation.

Incised Wounds

Incised wounds generally are longer than they are deep. As a sharp force injury, the tissues are cut, leaving sharp, clean edges unless the knife is dull or has attached ornamentation on the blade. Incised wounds are often present with stab wounds in a fatal knife attack. The most characteristic of these wounds is the hesitation wound seen in suicides and suicidal ideation and defense wounds or cuts seen when the victim attempts to ward off a knife attack.

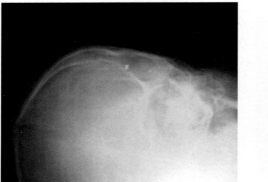

Figure 7.18 (a) Scissor fragment in skull. Radiographs are not only for gunshot wounds. In this x-ray of a stabbing victim, a small metallic fragment can be seen in the middle of the figure, a white dot near the top. This victim was stabbed with a scissors, part of which broke off in the skull. The small fragment was removed at the autopsy (see Figure 7.18b). Knife tips can break off when hitting bone as well. The broken fragment can be matched to a purported weapon. (b) Metallic fragment removed at autopsy. This is the scissors fragment removed as described in Figure 7.18a.

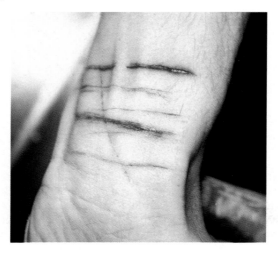

Figure 7.19 Incised wounds of the wrist (hesitation cuts). Incised wounds are longer than they are deep. These characteristic incised wounds of the wrist, seen in suicide attempts, are also called hesitation cuts.

Hesitation Marks or Wounds

Hesitation marks are commonly shallow incised wounds on the wrists and neck, although other areas such as the antecubital fossa (inside of the elbow) can be involved also. (Figure 7.19). These areas are sensitive parts of the body, so each cut is painful. When the person gets up enough nerve, another cut is made. Lack of determination and/or knowledge of anatomy means the cuts are not deep enough to hit vital arteries or veins, such as the radial artery in the wrist. In the author's experience, these wounds are not usually successful in causing death. The victim either survives (and forms linear scars) or resorts to another method of suicide, such as a drug overdose.

Defense Wounds or Cuts

Defense wounds are cuts, usually incised wounds of the hands, arms, shoulders, wrists, or even the upper thighs, sustained as a result of fighting off a knife attack (Figure 7.20). The victim might attempt to grab a knife, or block the knife blows with the arm. These cuts can be quite deep, severing tendons and muscles.

The word "defense" in defense wounds can be a misnomer because these wounds can be sustained if the deceased was the aggressor and simply lost the fight.

Puncture Wounds

Puncture wounds are usually deep wounds with a punctate (pointlike) entrance wound on the skin. Nails, awls, ice picks, and screwdrivers are typical weapons. Often, the side of the weapon will cause an abrasion that at least partially surrounds the wound. To cause death, many such wounds must be concentrated in a certain area, such as the heart (Figure 7.21).

Chopping Wounds

Chopping wounds are produced by weapons with at least one sharp edge, such as a machete, hatchet, axe, or meat cleaver (Figure 7.22a,b). These instruments are large and have weight, which can cause blunt force injuries as well, such as contusions and bone fractures.

Firearms and Gunshot Wounds

Firearms

Firearms fire a bullet or other projectile with tremendous kinetic energy, that when contacting the body, the kinetic energy is transferred to the skin, soft tissues, and organs. This energy produces a laceration of the tissues, including blood vessels, resulting in hemorrhage (the primary mechanism of death in many gunshot wound deaths). Other effects of gunshot wounds depend on the region of the body or organ system that is shot. Bullets striking the brain

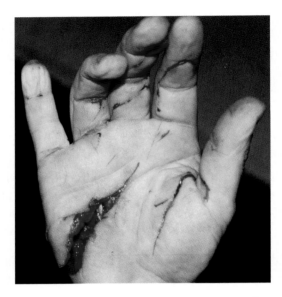

Figure 7.20 Incised wounds of the hand (defense cuts). Defense cuts are a special type of incised wound encountered when the victim attempts to fight off a knife attack. The deep cuts seen here tell us the story of the violence inherent in the attack, and the determination of the victim to prevent the attack.

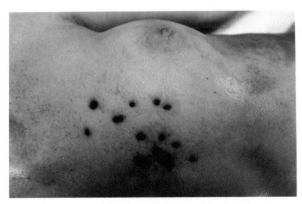

Figure 7.21 Puncture wounds of the chest. The victim was killed with an ice pick. The multiple stab wounds are located around the heart. The purposeful placement of the ice pick wounds around the heart display the determination of the perpetrator, that is, these are not randomly placed puncture wounds.

can cause laceration of vital parts of the brain, leading to near-immediate death. Gunshot wounds of the lungs can cause an air leak (pneumothorax) and subsequent death if untreated. The ferocity of gunshot wounds is such that the victim can survive the initial gunshot wound, only to die months later due to an infection or blood clot.

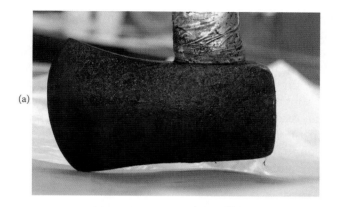

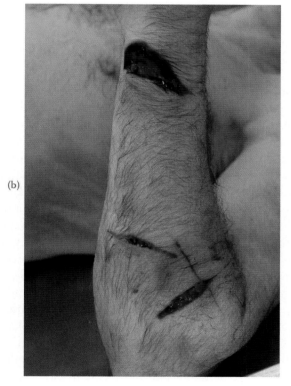

Figure 7.22 Chopping injuries: (a) axe and (b) axe wounds. Axes, swords, machetes, and other such weapons have sharp edges and weight. These weapons can cut, tear, and break bones. The cuts are often long and deep, as in (b). An axe can cause blunt force injuries and sharp force injuries. The wrist wound depicted in (b) shows abraded margins such as a laceration.

For many reasons, the firearm is unique among devices that can cause death. Unlike knives and blunt objects, a person can be killed without close contact. If a pattern is visible on the skin or clothing, an accurate estimate can be made of the firing distance. If the projectile (except for smoothed bore guns) can be found, the exact weapon can be identified. A person can shoot himself or be shot by another person and the wound is identical. For this reason, the author recommends performing autopsies in all suicides by gunshot. Also, to further document the purported suicide, the bullet can be retrieved for comparison to the gun.

The common types of civilian firearms include:

- Revolver
- Pistol
- Rifle
- Shotgun
- Machine gun

The pistol and revolver are commonly called handguns. The revolver most commonly holds six rounds (unfired bullets) in the central cylinder. The cylinder turns as the gun is fired. The pistol is loaded by a magazine, or clip, that may hold from seven to fifteen or more rounds. Rifles and shotguns are fired from the shoulder. Rifles vary greatly in the caliber and type of round that can be fired. Bullets from high-powered rifles fragment in the body, dispersing energy and causing a characteristic "lead snowstorm" on x-ray (Figure 7.23). Handguns and rifles have riflings, which cut unique lands and grooves in the bullet, specific to the exact gun that fired the weapon. Shotguns are smooth bored guns that generally shoot shot (or BBs). Some shotguns, particularly those for deer hunting, do have riflings for shooting a large projectile called a slug. The riflings make the gun more accurate by causing the bullet to spin.

Handguns and rifles fire ammunition or cartridges composed of a primer, gunpowder or propellant, and a bullet or projectile. When a firing pin of a weapon strikes the primer, the resulting explosion ignites the gunpowder. Gunpowder, vaporized primer, and metal from a gun may be deposited on the skin and/or clothing of the victim. In addition, elements from the primer may be deposited on objects in close proximity to a discharged weapon.

Gunpowder comes out of the muzzle in two forms:

1. Completely burned gunpowder, called "soot" or "fouling," can be washed off the skin (Figure 7.24).
2. Particles of burning and unburned powder can become embedded in the skin or bounce off and abrade the skin. The marks on the skin are called "tattooing" or "stippling."

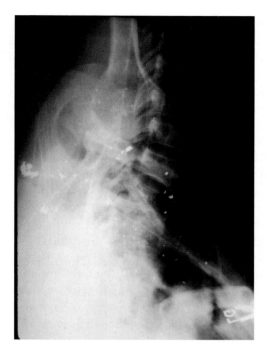

Figure 7.23 "Lead snowstorm." This lateral film of the neck shows metallic flakes in a complete path through the neck area. This person was shot with a high-powered rifle.

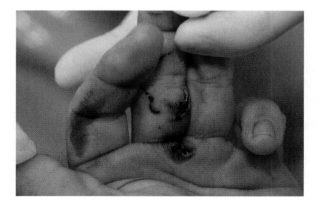

Figure 7.24 Gun-induced laceration and soot deposition of the hand. The mechanism of the pistol produced a laceration of the hand. Soot was also deposited on the hand and fingers. These findings indicated that the gun was in the hand of the victim and supports the theory of suicide. (Also see Figure 7.25.)

Gunshot Wounds

Inspecting the skin or the clothing for the characteristic patterns of burned and unburned gunpowder allows the wound to be classified by type as:

- *Hard contact (close contact):* The muzzle has been pushed tight or "hard" against the skin, forming a tight seal between the muzzle and skin, causing the heat, soot, and bullet to go into the wound. The result is most often charring of the wound edges (due to a heat of about 1400°F) and an abrasion of the wound margin. In bony areas where the skin is stretched, such as the forehead, the wound margins can tear, forming a stellate (starlike) pattern. Soot is then heavily deposited inside the wound. Backspatter may be present on the weapon or shooter (Figure 7.25).
- *Contact (loose contact):* The muzzle is incompletely or not quite touching the skin, so a slight rim of soot surrounds the wound. This soot can be washed away, and no stippling is seen. Less abrasion is present compared to a hard contact wound (Figure 7.26).
- *Near contact:* The muzzle is not touching the skin at all, but is within less than about 1 inch. A wide rim of soot and seared skin surround the entrance bullet hole, much wider than with a contact wound. No stippling is seen, or the wound must be classified as intermediate range (Figure 7.27).
- *Intermediate range:* Seeing stippling or powder tattooing of the skin is diagnostic of this wound (Figure 7.28). These wounds occur at muzzle-to-target distances of approximately 6 inches up to 3 or 4 feet, depending on the weapon used and the type of ammunition. There is no soot deposition or charring, only stippling or powder tattooing of the skin. Stippling is embedded in the skin and cannot be washed off. An estimate of the range of fire can be given if the diameter of the stippling on the body (or clothing) is compared to that of the weapon when test fired by a firearms examiner.
- *Distant (undetermined range):* No soot or stippling is seen. The wound has a small "abrasion collar" produced by the bullet scraping the skin circumferentially as the skin is perforated (Figure 7.29).

Exit Wounds   Exit wounds vary greatly in appearance. They can be irregular, stellate (Figure 7.30), slitlike, and rarely, round. Round exit wounds can resemble entrance wounds before they are cleaned. Exit wounds do not have an associated circular abrasion at the entrance hole. While exit wounds are generally larger than entrance wounds, some exit wounds are the same size or smaller. The death scene investigator (DSI) should be very cautious in giving an opinion about entrance and exit wounds at the scene where the lighting is often bad and the wounds are bloody. Opinions about gunshot wounds should only be given after a complete autopsy.

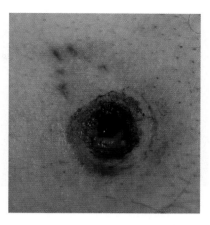

Figure 7.25 Hard-contact entrance gunshot wound. The patterned abrasion at 10 o'clock and the red abrasion ring around the wound were produced by the gun barrel and sight contacting the skin when the gun was fired. Around the wound is heavy soot, the black material. The finding of a hard-contact wound on the chest of this individual supports the theory of suicide.

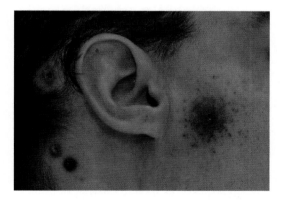

Figure 7.26 Loose-contact gunshot wound. The gunshot wound in the lower left-hand corner of the photo shows surrounding soot. The gun muzzle was held slightly away from the skin, causing soot to go into and around the wound. The wound in front of the ear shows a soot pattern that is wider and begins to break up, causing stippling, otherwise known as an intermediate range wound. The other two wounds behind and below the ear show no soot or stippling, so the range is classified as "undetermined" for these two wounds.

Shored Exit Wounds These are exit wounds with associated irregular abrasions that are caused by the skin contacting a hard surface (e.g., floor) or a tough article of clothing (e.g., leather coat).

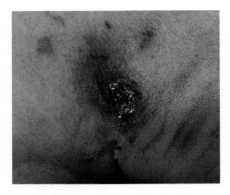

Figure 7.27 Near-contact wound. The term is used by some authors to describe a pattern between a contact and intermediate range wound. A wide rim of soot surrounds the wound because the barrel is not touching the skin and is likely less than an inch away. If stippling is seen, the wound must be classified as an intermediate range gunshot wound.

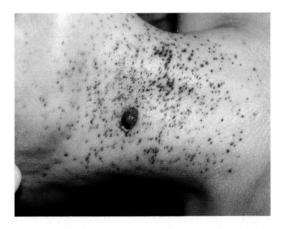

Figure 7.28 Intermediate-range gunshot wound. Any gunshot wound with stippling (small dots surrounding the wound) is referred to as an intermediate-range gunshot wound. Unburned portions of gunpowder tattoo the skin. The stippling must be measured in all directions. The firearms examiner can then fire test patterns with the same gun and ammunition at known distances. These patterns can be compared to the unknown pattern on the body, and the distance estimated.

Graze and Tangential Wounds   When a bullet strikes the skin at an angle insufficient for penetration into the deep subcutaneous tissue, the skin is torn and abraded. The tears often point in the direction the bullet traveled (Figure 7.31).

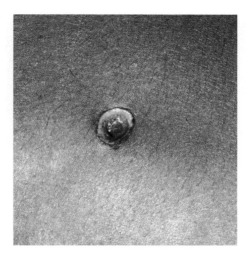

Figure 7.29 Undetermined-range gunshot wound. This gunshot wound has no surrounding soot or stippling; therefore, the range cannot be determined.

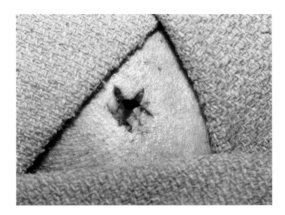

Figure 7.30 Exit wound. This exit wound is stellate in configuration. No soot or abrasion can be seen around the exit wound. This exit wound was caused by a .22-caliber bullet.

Secondary Target Wounds and Trace Evidence   If the bullet goes through any object before hitting the victim, parts of this object may be carried into the wound. For example, if the victim is shot through a blanket, a portion of blanket may be in the wound or stuck in the surrounding skin (Figure 7.32). Glass and clothing are common secondary targets.

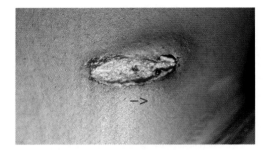

Figure 7.31 Graze wound. As the wound tangentially contacts the skin, it is abraded and torn. The tears point to the direction the bullet travels over the skin (as shown by the arrow).

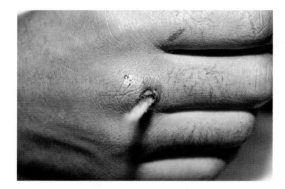

Figure 7.32 Intermediate target in a gunshot wound. This person was shot while holding up a blanket. The filling of the blanket was carried into the gunshot wound.

Shotgun Wounds

Shotguns fire shot, producing a dispersed pattern, the width of which depends on the choke of the gun (Figure 7.33). The shotgun wound produces additional wounds that give information regarding the range of fire. While the soot and stippling patterns are similar to those described above, the spread of the shot and the wounding pattern also can aid in estimating the range of fire. Portions of the shotgun shell packing (wadding) can also be found in the wound, up until a range of fire of about 5 to 6 feet. Patterns of shotgun wounds can be generally described as follows:

- *Contact to about 2 feet*: A single, round entrance hole is seen with all shot and wadding found within the wound.
- *2 to 4 feet*: The shot begin to disperse and a single irregular, scalloped "rat hole" is seen. Wadding is usually found in the wound.

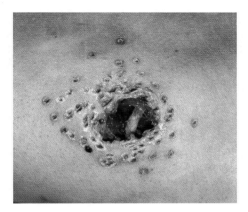

Figure 7.33 Shotgun wound. Shotgun shells contain multiple small BBs, called "shot." As the shot comes out of the barrel of the gun, it stays together for several feet and then starts to separate. As these individual shot break up and hit the skin, characteristic individual satellite shot injuries can be seen around the main hole.

- *4 feet to about 10 feet:* The shot disperse further with satellite holes surrounding the central hole. The wadding is probably not in the wound but might cause an abrasion if it strikes the skin.
- *10 feet and beyond:* The shot have dispersed such that a central hole is no longer seen, only individual entry wounds of each shot.

Shotguns that fire slugs may or may not be rifled. Once a slug enters the body, it usually does not exit. Riflings are only seen on those shotguns that are used to fire a slug. If the shotgun shell is found, firing pin tool marks can be matched to the shotgun in some cases.

Description of Wounds

At the autopsy, after the body is examined initially, the wounds are cleaned carefully. Each wound is photographed, measured, and diagrammed by the pathologist. The pathologist should include the wound track (path through the body), along with a three-dimensional description of the bullet path. The bullet is recovered by the pathologist, and then photographed, taking care not to damage the riflings on removal.

Miscellaneous Firearm and Gunshot Wound Facts

- *The caliber of the wound cannot be predicted by the size of the entrance wound.* Wound size can vary, depending on the energy of the bullet, the type of bullet, and the region of the body struck.

- *All gunshot wound cases should be x-rayed.* Even if there is an exit wound, x-rays should be performed. Part of the bullet, such as the jacket (which can contain riflings), can and often does remain in the body. The body should be x-rayed with the clothing on because clothing can trap bullets (Figure 7.34). Cartridge casings have been found in the hair at autopsy (Figure 7.35a,b)
- *The scene must be examined for bullets and cartridges.* In many jurisdictions, this is performed by law enforcement or crime scene technicians. It is useful to hold the crime scene until after the autopsy because after the complete examination of the wounds, some bullets might be missing.

Asphyxia

Asphyxia is a general term that refers to lack of oxygen for the cells of the tissues of the body, supreme of which is the brain. The lack of oxygen availability to the brain results in unconsciousness, and ultimately death in minutes. Suffocation is a type of asphyxia due to the lack of oxygen reaching the *blood*. Asphyxia can be classified as follows:

- *Compression of the neck:* hanging and strangulation
- *Chemical asphyxia:* for example, carbon monoxide, hydrogen cyanide

Figure 7.34 Bullet in a sweater. Some articles of clothing can trap bullets. For this reason, the clothing should be x-rayed and carefully searched, so as not to lose a bullet or other trace evidence.

Figure 7.35 Cartridge casing in the hair. The hair should be examined carefully for evidence. As shown here, a missing cartridge casing was found; and at about 8 o'clock, a bullet jacket can be seen in the clothing.

- *Suffocation:* lack of environmental oxygen, choking, and smothering
- *Postural or mechanical asphyxia:* compression of the chest

Compression of the Neck

Types of Hanging

There are two types of hanging: (1) judicial and (2) ligature. Judicial hangings are conducted by a strong rope or other strong material made to form a noose. Judicial hanging involves a free fall of many feet intended to cause a high cervical fracture, injuring the spinal cord and causing death. Ligature hangings are usually suicides, or "autoerotic," and are only rarely homicidal.

Ligature Hanging   In ligature hanging, the neck is compressed by rope, wire, or articles of clothing. The ligature begins to exert pressure on the neck, which initially occludes the vasculature. It takes about 4 to 7 pounds of pressure to occlude the jugular veins and about 11 to 12 pounds of pressure to occlude the carotid arteries (DiMaio, V.J.M. and Dana, S.E., 2006). The trachea is held open by strong cartilage in the anterior and lateral aspects, so it is not compressed unless the ligature is extremely tight. Tracheal compression is not needed to cause death, and is usually not seen in ligature hangings. The weight of the body, or even the head, is sufficient to cause death.

The body may be hanging free, touching the ground, or even slumped forward. Because blood cannot return to the heart normally, the face is blue due to congestion. The tongue may be protruding. Petechiae are seen in the conjunctiva in some cases. Ruptured blood vessels resembling large petechiae are often seen in the skin, especially in the lower extremities, and are called "Tardieu spots."

The ligature compresses and abrades the neck, causing an injury known as a "ligature furrow." The furrow is at least as wide as the ligature (Figure 7.36). The abrasion is often patterned, leaving an impression of the ligature. If possible, the ligature should be cut at the hanging point and left attached to the neck. The knot should not be untied. The pathologist will cut the ligature away from the neck at the autopsy.

Autoerotic Neck Compression or "Hanging"   Autoerotic deaths refer to the practice of occluding the jugular veins of the neck by oneself to experience pleasure during masturbation, usually with a ligature, resulting in death. These victims are usually male, and the diagnosis is readily made at the scene because the decedent may be naked and pornographic material is usually found nearby. The ligature apparatus can be elaborate, and provides some escape mechanism. Because unconsciousness can occur in 15 to 20 seconds, the victim can mistakenly pass out and later asphyxiate (Spitz, W.U., 2004). A towel or soft device is often placed between the ligature and neck to prevent abrasions. Often, there is evidence of repeated behavior at the scene,

Figure 7.36 Ligature around the neck from suicidal hanging. The ligature furrow is easily seen in this figure and the rope has caused a patterned abrasion of the neck.

such as grooves worn in the rafters where ropes or pulleys have been placed. The manner of death is "accident."

Types of Strangulation

There are two types of strangulation: (1) ligature and (2) manual. Ligature strangulation is nearly always homicidal; however, a tie or similar article can become caught in machinery or other objects and pull the ligature tight enough to cause death. The latter types of cases are often obvious at the scene. Manual strangulation commonly involves more and varied trauma to the neck.

Ligature Strangulation   In ligature strangulation, a weight other than the body's weight is used to compress the neck vasculature. In the majority of cases, the perpetrator manually tightens the ligature. There may be marks on the neck from the victim's own hands, attempting to resist. Petechiae seem to be more prominent than in other ligature deaths.

Manual Strangulation   Manual strangulation refers to applying pressure to the neck by the hands or forearms, usually compressing the vessels of the neck, causing injury, unconsciousness, or death. When extreme pressure is exerted on the neck, or in young victims, the airway can be compressed. Abrasions and contusions of the neck, jaw, tongue base, and even the mouth are often seen (Figure 7.37). Facial and conjunctival petechiae are often seen and the face is congested. The neck and tongue should be carefully dissected

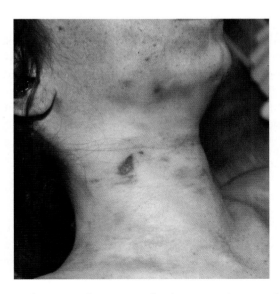

Figure 7.37 Manual strangulation. Multiple contusions and abrasions are seen at the base of the jaw and in the neck. Neck dissection showed extensive hemorrhage of the soft tissues and muscle of the anterior neck and base of the tongue.

by the pathologist and usually reveal muscle hemorrhage, hyoid and thyroid cartilage fracture, and other soft tissue hemorrhage. Semilunar fingernail-like abrasions can be present.

Chemical Asphyxia

Chemical asphyxia describes substances that interfere with the delivery of oxygen at the cellular level. Chief among these is carbon monoxide (CO), which when inhaled becomes carboxyhemoglobin. This molecule replaces oxygen on the hemoglobin molecule and impairs release of oxygen to the tissues. Carbon monoxide is a colorless and odorless gas that is a byproduct of the combustion of fossil fuel, wood, and other carbon-containing compounds. Carbon monoxide poisoning is commonly seen in the types of examples listed below:

- *Suicide:* Running a combustion engine and breathing the exhaust. The circumstances must be carefully evaluated to rule out an accident.
- *Accident:* Faulty furnace, water heater, space heater, or some other faulty home appliance is not properly vented and allows CO to be inhaled.
- *Smoke inhalation:* Among the causes of death in fires is the inhalation of smoke, which contains CO. Carbon monoxide is usually part of the mechanism of death in fires, which includes inhalation of very hot air and soot, as well as a lack of oxygen in the environment.

CO poisoning causes a progression of symptoms, based on the age, health, and percent of CO in the blood. Smokers can have up to 10% of CO in the blood. CO levels below 20%, which may only cause headaches, nausea, and vomiting in healthy adults, may cause death in children or those adults with heart or lung disease. In healthy adults, 50% CO is often fatal. In CO poisoning, the livor, tissue, and blood appear cherry red. Poisoning due to hydrogen cyanide and cold temperatures causes a pink lividity.

Suffocation

Suffocation is the lack of oxygen in the blood. Suffocation can be due to blockage of the airways, such as choking (or smothering), or a lack of oxygen in the environment, such as a poorly ventilated silo or mineshaft.

Choking

Choking is the blockage of the airway, due to a foreign object in the airway, or some alteration of the tissues of the airway, such as edema. Choking does not refer to strangulation. Food or foreign objects can obstruct the airways in adults or children. In adults, intoxication or debilitation creates a greater risk for choking. Acute epiglottitis (Figure 7.38), due to a bacterial infection, can obstruct the airway.

Smothering

Smothering is the covering of the mouth (or trachea) and nose. This can be done by simply using the hand in children, or by using gags, tape, or tight plastic bags in adults who may be bound or restrained (Figure 7.39). Adults who are manually smothered often have mouth and lip injuries due to struggling. Smothering can be accidental in infants due to bedding or other objects around the house covering the mouth and nose. Homicidal smothering of an infant is very difficult to detect from examination. Even petechiae can be difficult to see in such cases.

Lack of Oxygen in the Environment: "Environmental Asphyxia"

Humans require at least 9% oxygen in the air to breathe normally. When oxygen levels drop, the individual begins to suffer form hypoxia. In fires, the oxygen is consumed by the fire. In some cases, other gases displace oxygen and functionally cause a hypoxic environment. In the use of "whippets" with a plastic bag (Figure 7.40a,b,c), nitrous oxide replaces oxygen, causing a hypoxia in the bag. Poorly ventilated mine shafts can become hypoxic. These environments are very hazardous to the death investigation team, and entry to the scene should not be made until experts declare the area safe.

Figure 7.38 Epiglottitis. Edema and swelling of the epiglottis can cause occlusion of the airway and death. The rounded, meaty-red, swollen epiglottis shown here was the result of group B *Streptococcus* infection. The victim had trouble breathing and died suddenly after having a severe sore throat for several days.

Figure 7.39 Smothering. A plastic bag was placed over the head and a gag was placed in the mouth of this individual. Tying the hands subdued the victim such that he could not remove the devices causing the smothering.

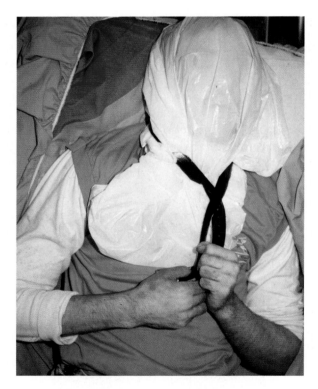

Figure 7.40 Nitrous oxide use causing suffocation. (a) This individual used the depicted nitrous oxide canisters from a whipped cream dispenser (b and c) to release the gas into a plastic bag. This bag was placed over his head, as shown in (a). Note the belt, which was used to cinch the bag closed. The nitrous oxide replaces the oxygen in the bag, causing asphyxia. Nitrous oxide is a recreational drug that causes euphoria, a floating feeling, and laughter.

Contains pure N₂O under
pressure. Store in a cool
and dry place.
Do not inhale. Misuse
can be dangerous to
your health. Keep
out of reach of children.
Made in Hungary

Figure 7.40 Continued

Mechanical and Positional Asphyxia

The diaphragm and chest wall must be able to rise and fall for a person to inhale air. If this action is restricted mechanically or by the position of the person, asphyxia occurs. This effect can be enhanced by intoxication. Mechanical asphyxia is seen in motor vehicle crashes as the individual is tightly wedged in the wreck vehicle. Also, the "shade-tree mechanic" who has a car fall on him due to a faulty jack can suffer mechanical asphyxia. Infants who are in the bed with adults can be the victims of "overlay." This is when the child is overlain by the heavier adult while the adult is sleeping. Intoxication of the adult can make this scenario more likely. Children can be wedged into beds, couches, or bedding as well.

Individuals can be trapped or placed into positions where breathing is difficult. An example of this is when a person is suspended upside down for some period of time. Crucifixion suspends the body such that breathing is difficult and labored, eventually resulting in asphyxia.

Drowning

Drowning is an asphyxial death in which the lack of oxygen is due to water (or other liquid) in the airways. The water occupies space in the airways and lungs, and does not allow for the effective exchange of oxygen. In freshwater drowning, water is drawn into the lungs, while in salt water, the blood plasma is drawn out of the lungs. In either case, there is severe damage to the lungs, which results in lack of oxygen to the brain and death. If the person is rescued (called "near drowning" by some), complications include pulmonary edema, pneumonia, irreversible hypoxic brain injury and death. During the drowning process, one inhales and also often swallows water. However, if a dead body is thrown in the water, the stomach and lungs can be filled with water.

Drowning should be considered when a body is found in the following situations:

- In water: other causes should be ruled out (e.g., homicide)
- Near water or tub
- A wet body having water marks or other indications of being wet

There are no reliable, objective drowning tests to prove drowning. Mastoid bone hemorrhage, blood electrolyte analysis, and diatom studies have been shown to be inconclusive. Drowning, when suspected, is diagnosed by excluding other causes of death. For this reason, all drowning cases must be autopsied to rule out natural and violent causes of death. Some findings are consistently seen in, but not diagnostic of, drowning, including:

- *Foam cone:* white foam exuding from the mouth and nose.
- *"Washerwoman hands":* wet wrinkling of the hands due to saturation with water. This is reversible and can occur after death.
- *Water in the stomach:* can indicate that water was swallowed in acute drowning.

Occasionally, marine life, more often in salt water, may feed on the skin of the face, especially around the mouth, nose, and ears. Pre- or postmortem abrasions may be found on the forehead, knees, and backs of hands from the body scraping against the bottom of the lake or pool.

Electrocution

In electrocution, the history and circumstances of death are vitally important because low-voltage deaths frequently cause no injuries on the body. On the other hand, high-voltage deaths are easier to diagnose because of obvious burns.

The cause of death from electrocution is related to the amount of current (or amperage) flowing through a body. Although both direct and alternating currents can be lethal, most deaths occur from contact with alternating currents having low voltages, such as 110 or 220 volts usually found in homes.

There needs to be a complete circuit from the power source to the ground for death to occur. A person will not become electrocuted if insulated from the ground. The direction the path takes in the body determines whether shock will be fatal. An arrhythmia is likely if current travels through the heart.

External injuries can vary tremendously. The extent of external wound damage depends on the amount of current and its duration. If a current spreads over a wide contact area for a short duration, there will not be any injuries to the skin. Clothing may be damaged so it must be retained for examination. The skin may be secondarily injured by burning clothes.

Low voltage tends to cause easily overlooked small burns, especially on the hands and the feet. The lesions can be peripherally red, black, or white and inconspicuous, with depressed firm white centers (Figure 7.41).

High-voltage deaths usually leave easily recognizable, deeply charred areas. Lesions may be present at the entrance and/or exit sites. If a death occurs due to working with electrical equipment, the equipment should be tested by a qualified individual. If a body is found near wires, or in the service area of a house (e.g., crawl space), electrocution should be suspected. The death investigation team should exercise caution if electrocution is suspected until the source of electricity is identified and neutralized.

Lightning

Lightning is a high-current electrical discharge that can kill by either a direct or an indirect strike. Direct strikes cause thousands of amperes of current to flow through the body, causing cardiac arrest. Indirect strikes are from current arcing or being conducted to the person, usually by metallic objects.

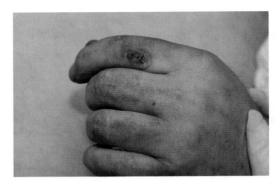

Figure 7.41 Electrical injury, index finger. The point of entry or exit of electrical current traveling through the body often results in a burn. The burn shows central charring with a surrounding red area. A history of an electrician working on electrical equipment prompts a search for such an injury. The sole of the foot is another common site of injury. Some electrocutions show no external injuries.

Injuries may be slight to nonexistent or quite impressive. Metal on the clothing or body may heat up and cause secondary injuries.

Occasionally, a red, fernlike pattern may develop on the skin. This ferning pattern is only seen in electrocution and may disappear within hours of the death. Other patterns of injury include rupture of the eardrums and tattering of clothing. Consider lighting as a cause of death when a person is found dead outside in the appropriate conditions, remembering lighting can occur both in and *near* thunderstorms.

Fire Deaths and Thermal Injuries

Most fire deaths are due to smoke inhalation, not direct thermal injury. Exposure to smoke and its main poison, CO, can be fatal within minutes. Thermal effects to the body may be slight or severe. The degree of heat does not dictate how long a person survives during a fire. The extent of damage depends on the length of time a decedent is exposed to flames and how close a body is to a fire.

The most important factor in any fire death investigation is determining whether an individual was dead before the fire started (suspected homicide). This is determined by examining the airway for the inhalation of smoke and the measurement of CO content in the blood. These evaluations can only be determined in the morgue.

CO will cause cherry-red livor mortis. Occasionally, the blood CO will be negative, as it is in an explosion or a very hot fire that causes death rapidly. A negative CO might initially be confusing, but a scene investigation by fire officials should reveal the nature of the fire.

Individuals may die later in the hospital from complications such as inhalation injuries to the airways, infections, and fluid and electrolyte disorders. Skin burns may range from partial or full thickness to charring and incineration.

Heat artifacts include:

- Changes in height and weight of the body.
- Changes in hair color. Brown hair may become red, and blonde hair may become gray. Black hair does not change color.
- Thermal fractures. These are difficult to differentiate from antemortem fractures.
- Skin splits with evisceration of organs.
- Most fire deaths should be x-rayed so that foreign objects will not be overlooked. Blood can usually be obtained from a body regardless of how badly it is burned.

Hyperthermia

Very few signs at autopsy will indicate that a person died from hyperthermia. The most important sign is body temperature. If a body is found at a scene soon after death, an increased temperature will be evident. If a decedent is not found for many hours, or is discovered the next day, a diagnosis may be impossible.

There are a number of causes of hyperthermia. Older people may succumb to heat during summer months because of an underlying disease that contributes to their inability to cope with heat, or their dwellings may not have an appropriate cooling system. Malignant hyperthermia is a syndrome that develops in people who react to certain drugs, such a phenathiazines (thorazine) or halothane. The use of cocaine and methamphetamine are also associated with hyperthermia. In some of these cases, there is a genetic predisposition toward developing malignant hyperthermia.

Hypothermia

Hypothermia occurs more commonly in those individuals who have underlying disease or are incapacitated, such as under the influence of alcohol. People can die from improperly heated homes or apartments or if they are caught outside in the cold. Alcoholics can become hypothermic if they fall asleep in the cold while inebriated. Nursing-home patients can succumb to the cold after becoming confused and walking outdoors during winter months.

There are usually no external signs of trauma unless the individual was rendered incapacitated by an injury before dying from the cold.

"Paradoxical undressing" may occur because the individual may begin to undress while dying from the cold. This may appear suspicious if the decedent is a naked woman found outside with her clothes strewn about. An initial impression may suggest a sexual assault; however, further investigation should uncover the correct manner and cause of death.

Motor Vehicle Occupant Injuries

When a motor vehicle is involved in an accident, the driver and passengers will travel toward the site of the impact. For example, an impact to the front left of a car during a head-on crash will cause occupants to move to the left, especially if unrestrained. The driver may hit the steering wheel, dashboard, or windshield, and the passenger may hit the dashboard, windshield, or rearview mirror. Each may have significant injuries although they hit different objects.

There may be few external marks when there are seat belts and airbags; however, internally, there may be impressive injuries to the heart and aorta. Seat belt abrasions on the shoulder and hips are common. The location of the marks helps differentiate between the driver and the passenger.

Side-window glass causes a characteristic injury because it is made of tempered glass, which will shatter into numerous small fragments upon impact. These fragments will cause a characteristic "dicing" pattern of lacerated abrasions on the face, shoulders, and/or arms. A driver will have dicing injuries on the left side of the body and a passenger will have them on the right side of the body.

Other common injuries involve fractures of the patella (knee) and femur caused by hitting the dashboard and the extremities caught under the seat. High-speed collisions can cause multiple severe injuries. There may be extensive skull fractures and facial lacerations, contusions, and abrasions. Common injuries to the trunk include rib and pelvic fractures with associated internal injuries. Lacerations of these internal organs may occur without associated rib fractures. If any of the occupants are ejected during a crash, obviously the injuries can be quite variable and very severe. Head trauma is common in these situations. In addition, when an occupant is ejected, a vehicle may roll over and compress the occupants, causing compressive asphyxia, often with few other injuries.

Pedestrian Injuries

In a hit-and-run pedestrian fatality, a study of the injuries may help identify the vehicle. The points of impact on a body are particularly important and clothing must be closely examined for paint chips and parts of the vehicle that may be transferred on impact. Bumper impact sites on the legs should be measured from the heel. This may indicate the bumper height. A bumper fracture is often triangular in shape with the apex of the triangle pointing in the direction that a vehicle was moving. If a driver applied the brakes suddenly, a bumper fracture may be lower than expected because applying the brakes may drop the front end of the car. Adults tend to be run under while children, with lower centers of gravity, tend to be run over.

Investigation of Childhood Fatalities and Child Abuse

The investigation of deaths in children requires some experience and special training. The death of a child can be psychologically difficult for the death investigation team. Dealing with a distraught family under these circumstances can be especially difficult. Nonetheless, the investigation must continue so that the key question of a child death can be asked: Does the given history match the injuries or condition of the child? Because all children will have a parent, guardian, or some caretaker, someone is usually available to provide a history. The history or circumstances should be obtained from the person who found or was caring for the child when the death occurred. Many times, this history is obtained initially by medical personnel at the hospital. When the abuse is discovered, the parent or caretaker becomes a suspect and might refuse to be interviewed.

Child abuse is the physical or mental injury of a minor due to the act of omission or commission of a person responsible for the care and/or well-being of that child. In child abuse cases, it is very useful to interview the parent or caretaker as soon after the death as possible. In most cases of abuse, the injuries do not match the story that is given. In neglect cases, basic medical care or food may have been omitted, and there is no adequate explanation for this omission. The DSI and the pathologist should search diligently to rule out reasonable explanations for apparent abuse or neglect — that is, be objective. For example, failure to gain weight can be due to an undiagnosed medical condition.

Abuse and neglect cases have some common features, the most notable of which are:

- The history given does not match the injuries observed.
- No history is given; "I don't know" (not common; usually some story is given).
- The perpetrator often implicates himself in the fictitious account.

- There is often a delay in medical treatment. A family member or friend might be called instead of emergency medical services. The child may be taken from the scene to police or fire department.
- Multiple injuries over time, both old and new.
- Failure to seek appropriate care in the past.
- Inappropriate medical care or inadequate medical care rendered by the caretaker.
- Frequent visits to multiple doctors and emergency departments in multiple locations.
- Inappropriate response to the seriousness of a child's injury.
- Behavioral extremes and extreme mood swings in the child.
- Wariness of physical contact in the child.
- Previous child protective services calls.
- Health-care workers have previously missed injuries or the signs of abuse.

Battered-Child Syndrome

These children have a history of being repeatedly beaten by a caregiver. The injuries occur over a period of weeks, months, and/or years. Usually there are numerous injuries of different ages. Some of these injuries may be patterned (Figure 7.42). It is common to see a child with healing rib fractures and old contusions in addition to the recent injuries that caused the death. Blunt force injuries can be hidden and difficult to see externally (Figure 7.43). Head injuries from blunt trauma may only be visible on the undersurface of the scalp at autopsy. Contusions of the trunk may be readily apparent or absent

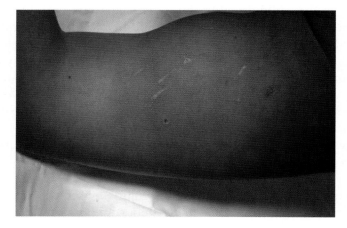

Figure 7.42 Abusive patterned injuries on the posterior thighs. The curved marks on the skin are marks from repeated whipping with a belt.

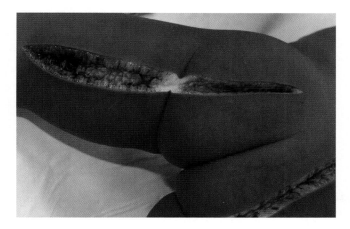

Figure 7.43 Incision into legs revealing hemorrhage. Deep contusions are difficult to see in children. Deep incisions may be necessary to reveal soft tissue hemorrhage.

even though there are fatal injuries to the internal organs. An autopsy is essential in these cases.

Shaken (Infant) Impact Syndrome

The shaken (infant) impact syndrome is a collection of injuries that results in severe brain injury, coma, and death. These injuries include or may include:

- Subdural hematoma (Figure 7.44)
- Retinal hemorrhage
- Scalp contusion (in many cases)
- Skull fracture (in few cases)

There is some controversy about whether violent shaking alone can cause tearing of the bridging veins in the subdural space and retinal hemorrhage. A skull fracture indicates a large amount of force. A visual contusion at autopsy indicates that blunt force was applied, imparting deceleration injury to the head. If the head is impacted on a soft surface, visual contusion may be absent. Some witness accounts and confessions seem to indicate that violent shaking can cause a subdural hematoma and retinal hemorrhage (Spitz, W.U., 2004).

Shaking a child or an infant may cause a fatal head injury without external marks. Violent shaking may cause nerve damage, brain swelling, and slight hemorrhage. Retinal hemorrhages may also occur, but these can

Figure 7.44 Subdural hematoma. Dark blood clot can be seen under the dura matter, which is held up in the photo.

only be seen with an ophthalmoscope. There may be contusions on the arms or chest where the infant was grabbed while being shaken.

A child usually becomes unconscious or noticeably abnormal within minutes of the violent act. Because there may be no obvious signs of abuse, emergency room personnel may not be suspicious of any foul play. An investigation should be conducted on any child who is dead on arrival or dies in the emergency room. If a child dies in an emergency room, the scene of injury should be visited and investigated.

Neglect, a Crime of Omission

Neglect is an abusive act of omission but can be no less lethal to a helpless child. For example, if a child is not fed or if a child is left in a harmful situation (like a hot car), death may occur. If a child is malnourished, his skin may be lax with little underlying soft tissue. He may appear underweight for his age, and the eyes may appear sunken. Vitreous humor will be sampled later at autopsy for chemical confirmation of dehydration. Sudden loss of weight can be determined by reviewing any previous medical records and comparing past-to-present weights. Failure to seek appropriate medical care is a form of neglect, and a sign of further abuse.

Sudden Infant Death Syndrome (SIDS)

A diagnosis of SIDS requires a complete autopsy and scene investigation; SIDS can only be diagnosed if both the scene and the autopsy are unremarkable. There is no provable cause of death.

Questions and observations of the scene include:

- Sleeping conditions. Was the child sleeping with the parents in their bed or in his own crib?
- Were there soft pillows or conditions in which the child could have suffocated on bedding or in between parts of the crib, bed, or other furniture?
- When was the child last seen and fed?
- There may be bloody fluid exuding from the mouth. This is commonly seen in a SIDS death.
- Do the caretaker's statements fit the body? Are livor and rigor appropriate for the reported times?

Identification Methods

8

Collection of Evidence at the Scene

Identification is one of the key functions and responsibilities of the medical examiner/coroner's (MEC) office. Establishing positive identification is important for a number of reasons. The goal is to produce a death certificate with the proper person's name. Most important is the next of kin. Denials of the death, as part of the grieving process, can be strong initially, especially for out-of-town family members. One can only imagine the problems that can arise if the wrong body is at the funeral. To receive death benefits, life insurance policies, and to proceed with the probate of wills, a positive identification is needed. Rarely, individuals do fake deaths for various reasons, such as to collect life insurance monies.

In criminal homicides and other criminal proceedings, the identity must be known in order to try the case. Rapid identification of the deceased allows detectives and other investigators to interview witnesses, family members, and associates of the deceased soon, while the crime is fresh.

The death scene investigator (DSI) must continually be aware of any situations in which misidentification can occur. The potential for misidentification is ever present at the scene of multiple fatalities and disasters, such as traffic fatalities where the remains are commingled. Care must be taken by taking as much time as needed to be certain of each identification and by using a second or supporting method if there is any doubt.

Visual Identification

This nonscientific method is the most easy and common way of performing an identification (ID). The family or even close friends or neighbors view the body and confirm the identity. This can also be done by taking a digital or a

111

Polaroid picture of the body. The DSI can help confirm the identification by looking at a picture or picture ID of the deceased. The driver's license is very good for this because height, weight, and eye color are noted. If the deceased is in surroundings (e.g., home, car, job, etc.) that are familiar and appropriate and the face is in good condition, the investigator can become comfortable with this method of ID. However, there may be pitfalls to this method.

Laypersons can become upset or uncomfortable at the sight of the body and might not look at the face. They might agree too quickly with the ID to simply get away from the body. People do not appear the same in death as compared to life. Witnesses can be deceptive, or claim to know the person. In cases of moderate decomposition or extensive facial injures, it might not be possible to make a good visual ID, and thus other methods must be used. In the final analysis, the MEC is responsible for the ID of the decedent; so if there is any doubt, other methods must be used.

Other Visual Methods of Identification

Scars, tattoos, birthmarks, moles, dentures (which often have the dentist's or the person's name etched within), other marks, jewelry, clothing, and other personal items can be used to support or, if unique enough, confirm the identification (Figure 8.1). These items are particularly useful when there is slight doubt in facial identification. It is always better to use several points of ID when using visual methods (e.g., facial, two hip replacement scars, and three unique tattoos on the body). One should keep in mind that all tattoos and non-medical scars are not unique. Unless the person has been incarcerated, there is probably not a good and/or complete description of these markings. Therefore, one must rely on family and friends for the description.

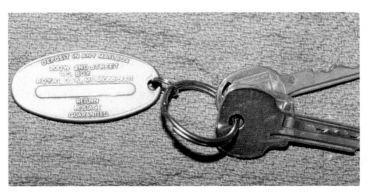

Figure 8.1 Keys found in victim's pocket. Personal effects that are unique can help confirm identity. These keys were marked with a unique serial number, registered to the individual (numbers sanitized).

Also, jewelry and clothing can be traded, changed, or stolen, so caution is advised in using clothing alone as an ID point.

"Softer" Forms of Identification

This includes information based on association and exclusion. For example, a person was burned up in a house fire. The person who lived there did not show up for work and is missing. This person fits the height, weight, and sex of the person living there. This information is important for an additional ID but should be backed up with more information if possible.

Scientific Forms of Identification

Scientific methods involve specific criteria agreed upon by experts to establish ID. These scientific methods are generally too time consuming or costly to perform in each death, nor are they necessary in each death. However, in cases involving homicides, severe decomposition, charred bodies, severe facial injuries, unusual or suspicious deaths, and multiple traffic or transit fatalities, at least one scientific method should be used to confirm the ID. Scientific forms of identification include:

- DNA analysis
- Fingerprints
- Dental identification
- Comparison of antemortem and postmortem x-rays
- Confirming a specific medical prosthesis

DNA Analysis

Since deoxyribonucleic acid (DNA) analysis became available in the middle 1980s, it has revolutionized identification procedures and criminal justice. Positive blood type analysis in the past could only be given in terms of a certain percent of the population. Currently, a positive DNA sample can statistically narrow down the identity of an individual to one in billions to a trillion. DNA analysis is not the answer for identifying all individuals and solving all crimes. The public may expect every crime and even every death investigation to include some sort of DNA analysis. Due to the expense, time, and the need for samples from parents or other relatives, DNA analysis is only used for identity in those cases when other forms of identification are not adequate.

Each person has a unique (unless there is an identical twin) collection of DNA within the nuclei of all cells. Mitochondrial DNA is the exception. Mitochondria are small organelles found in all cells, containing a small amount of DNA different from the large amounts found in the nuclei of cells. Mitochondrial DNA is passed *unchanged* from the mother to all her children. DNA is a long molecule with many sequences containing only four amino acids. In DNA analysis, the DNA is extracted from the sample, and then short sequences of DNA (i.e., short tandem repeats, or STRs) are replicated into many copies. These copies of short DNA sequences are then measured, producing a *profile*. The profile of the unknown person or *evidence sample* is compared to the standard sample.

When all the DNA sequences (DNA profiles) are identical, the results are reported as a "match." The result is also given weight in terms of how probable or how frequent a given DNA profile is found in a given population. This probability calculation gives the investigator or jury an idea of how much weight to assign to a given result.

Polymerase chain reaction (PCR) and the newer STR methods are much quicker and require less DNA than the older restriction fragment length polymorphism (RFLP) testing. The STR method is superior to the other methods because the fragments are small and easily amplified so that analysis can be performed on a very small amount of DNA or with degraded samples. In 1998, the FBI set up the Combined DNA Index System (CODIS), a database for DNA profiling of individuals based on 13 different STR loci. Mitochondrial DNA is used as a last resort, when the DNA is severely degraded. Mitochondrial DNA is more robust, and there are more copies in the cell than nuclear DNA.

Many MEC offices routinely store samples of blood indefinitely in all cases, on commercially available cards, so that the DNA can be analyzed if any future questions arise regarding identity, criminal involvement, or paternity.

Fingerprints

This method of identity has been in use for more than 100 years, and no two fingerprints have been shown to have identical ridge details — not even in identical twins. Fingerprinting is a quick, inexpensive method of identification. Many local police have fingerprint experts on staff or close by. Currently, the Automated Fingerprint Identification Systems (AFIS) is available online to law enforcement. The prints are scanned into the system, and by computer, can achieve results in minutes to hours as compared to the manual methods taking weeks to months. Printouts of potential matches from the system are extremely detailed but need final confirmation by a fingerprint expert.

The fingerprint identification method is useful as long as fingerprints are available for comparison. Generally, *antemortem* fingerprints are available for those individuals who were or are in the military, in some government positions, in the custody of law enforcement, holders of some licenses, and others (about 10% of the population). If no fingerprints are on file, personal items such as toothbrushes, hairbrushes, and the like can be used to make a postmortem comparison.

All homicides, suspicious deaths, and identity-problem cases should have a full set of classifiable prints taken (Figure 8.2).

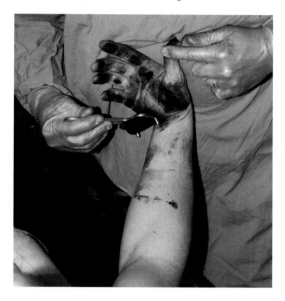

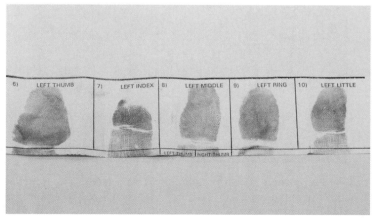

Figure 8.2 Postmortem fingerprints. It is essential that experienced technicians obtain postmortem fingerprints in all homicides, potential homicides, and suspicious deaths.

The victim must be fingerprinted to *exclude* his or her prints from those found at the scene. Some advocate a set of prints in all cases seen by an MEC office. Fingerprints can be lifted from all but the most severely burned or decomposed individuals.

Dental Identification

Comparing the dental examination of the body to antemortem dental records and/or x-rays by a forensic odontologist is a very reliable method of identification, but less so than fingerprints. As with fingerprints, some records (either charts and/or x-rays) must be available for comparison. Comparing antemortem dental charts is much less accurate than x-ray comparison. The charts can be old and out of date, causing inaccuracies. X-rays can show fillings, tooth root morphology, and sinuses, among other features. The forensic odontologist can give an opinion of a match when an acceptable number of features or points of identification correlate (Figure 8.3a,b).

X-Ray Comparisons and Medical Devices

If antemortem x-rays exist, certain comparisons with postmortem films may aid in identification. The sinuses of the skull can be useful to compare because the sinus configurations are thought to be unique. This author recommends another point of identification as well if sinuses are compared. Calcified regions or strictures in the body can form unique patterns and be found in unique areas. These include granulomas in the lung, calcified heart

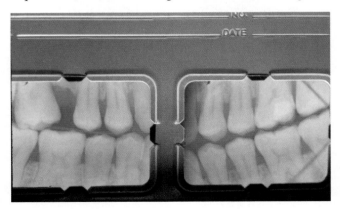

Figure 8.3 (a) Premortem dental radiographs. Premortem radiographs obtained from the dentist of the purported victim can be compared with autopsy dental radiographs. (b) Premortem dental charts. Pre-mortem dental charts can be compared with the teeth at autopsy to make an identification. Dental charts can be more important than x-rays because they may be more up-to-date.

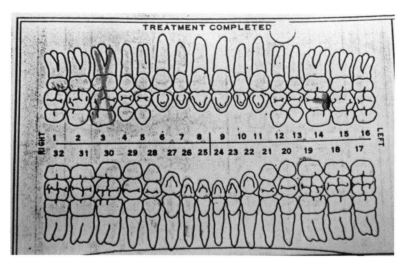

Figure 8.3 (b)

Figure 8.4 Hip prosthesis. The silver object in the center of the picture, inside the hole in the decomposing skin, is a hip prosthesis. Because serial numbers are recorded in the patient's medical records, the identity could be confirmed. If the manufacturer is known, it is possible to trace the recipient with some devices.

valves, and blood vessels. Previous fracture with orthopedic hardware in place can be specific for an individual if it is the type of device that carries a specific serial number (e.g., artificial hip or knee) (Figure 8.4). These serial numbers can be found in the medical record of the surgery. Other medical devices with serial numbers include breast implants, pacemakers, insulin pumps, and penile prostheses.

Crime Scene Evidence Collection

Scene Investigation and Specific Forms of Evidence

Crime scene technicians, a medical examiner or investigator, and law enforcement all take part in examining the scene for clues. The following is a list of different types of evidence that may be found at the scene, and how that evidence is usually collected and preserved. Most of these items are collected by the crime scene technician, who is responsible for the proper collection, documentation, and storage of the evidence. **The technician should be consulted before any evidence is handled.**

- *Blood.* Dried particles should be scraped into a dry container. Some dried areas may be sampled with a wet swab. The specimen should be dried before sealing it in a container. Articles of clothing or other objects containing blood may be submitted to a laboratory for a technician to remove.
- *Semen.* The article of clothing should be collected or the specimen on the clothing can be lifted with water or saline.
- *Fingerprints.* Soft objects containing an impression, such as clay, may be collected in their entirety. Prints on hard objects such as glass or furniture should be lifted at the scene.
- *Firearms and other weapons.* Firearms should be submitted to a lab without special treatment at the scene. The technician must ensure proper handling so that fingerprints are not smudged or ruined. The pathologist performing the autopsy may need to see a suspected weapon for comparison with injuries on the body. Great care should be taken not to contaminate firearms or any evidence that has not been processed.
- *Bullets and cartridges.* Bullets and cartridges should not be grasped with metal forceps because points of comparison may be damaged.
- *Hairs and fibers.* Hairs and fibers should be placed in separate containers and should not be crushed with a hard object such as metal tweezers.
- *Suspicious foods and pills.* Each item should be placed in a separate container or bag to prevent contamination.
- *Footprints and tire marks.* At the scene, casts should be made and close-up photographs should be taken with and without scale.
- *Tool marks.* There should be close-up photographs of the marks made by tools and, if possible, the damaged material should be removed for analysis by a lab technician.
- *Blood spatters.* Blood spatters should be photographed and described for analysis as to distance and angle of splatter. Samples may be removed for testing and preservation.

- *Miscellaneous.* Glass, soil, documents, cigarette butts, tobacco, and items thought to be involved in arson should all be collected and submitted to the fire department arson investigators. Items such as clothing can contain accelerant and should be stored in a sealed container such as a clean paint can.

Every scene should be diagrammed and photographed. Some jurisdictions are now using video in addition to still photography. Each item submitted to the lab should be referenced by either a photograph or written description as to its location in the scene. All containers with items submitted to the lab must be labeled with a case number, date, time, and name of the person who collected the specimen. Each specimen must have a chain of custody to determine who handled the specimen from the time it was initially packaged to the time it was stored after the analysis.

Signs of Cardiopulmonary Resuscitation and Treatment

9

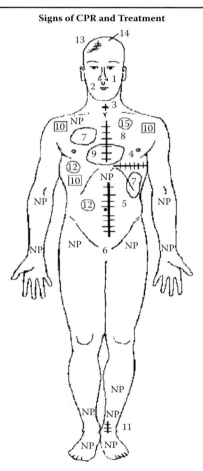

Figure 9.1 Signs of CPR and treatment. (*Source:* From Dix, J., *Handbook for Death Scene Investigators*, CRC Press, Boca Raton, FL, 1999. With permission.)

121

Key to Figure 9.1

1. *Nasogastric tube*: A flexible tube inserted into the mouth (or nose) to the stomach.
2. *Endotracheal tube:* A stiff tube inserted through the mouth or nose, through the larynx (voice box) into the trachea. A tight air seal and anchoring point is made by an inflatable balloon located at the base.
3. *Cricothyroidotomy and tracheotomy*: The cricothyroidotomy is an emergency procedure performed when injuries or other problems prevent the use of an endotracheal tube. The cricothyroid membrane is located approximately one finger breadth below the bottom of the protuberance of the larynx (Adam's apple). The cricothyroid membrane is thin and allows access to the airway without risk of cutting the thyroid gland or major blood vessels. Use of this procedure should be rare but its presence indicates extreme difficulty with a resuscitation. An endotracheal tube is usually inserted in the opening.

   A tracheotomy is a surgical procedure performed in the hospital. The tracheotomy is performed by a physician. It is an incision in the lower neck through the skin and airway (trachea) to establish an airway. This can be done emergently (under controlled surgical conditions) or more commonly for the patient with long-term breathing problems. A tracheostomy tube is inserted, which is much shorter than the endotracheal tube. The incision should not be confused with a stab or incised wound, although it can appear as such when the tracheostomy tube is removed.
4. *Thoracotomy*: These are large incisions made into the sides of the chest, usually on the left side below the nipple. They are made in an attempt to remove blood and to perform open cardiac massage.
5. *Laparotomy*: An incision into the abdominal cavity to check for blood and injuries.
6. *Foley catheter:* A tube to empty the bladder.
7. *Abrasions/burns from defibrillation (shock).*
8. *Sternotomy:* A midline incision into the chest and sternal bone to expose the heart.
9. *Contusions from chest compressions.*
10. *EKG (electrocardiogram) patches.*
11. *Cutdowns:* These are incisions in the skin made by scalpels. This method is used to obtain immediate access to a larger blood vessel. The objective is to locate a blood vessel into which a catheter can be inserted. Most of the time, a catheter is in the blood vessel and held there by a suture. Occasionally, the catheter and the suture material are not present. These cutdowns are more commonly located over the ankles, wrists, and front of the elbows (antecubital fossae).

12. *Chest tubes:* Chest tubes are inserted into the sides of the chest (lateral thorax or chest wall). The main purposes of a chest tube are to reinflate a collapsed lung and to remove blood from the chest cavity. The tubes are sewn into position, and once removed, can look like a stab wound. The medical record or treating physician should be consulted if there is any doubt.

13. *Craniotomy:* In trauma cases, the skull is opened to remove subdural and other blood from around the brain.

14. *Pressure monitors of the brain:* A steel device is placed through the scalp and skull to monitor the pressure of the brain during swelling and bleeding from trauma.

15. *Implanted defibrillators and pacing devices:* These small devices are surgically implanted under the skin in the upper chest. They may be done emergently in the operating room, or may be permanently implanted in patients with cardiac arrhythmias.

16. NP *Needle punctures:* These are needle puncture sites used for drawing blood and placement of intravenous catheters attached to fluid bags. Some of the catheters and fluid bags may still be in place. In addition to those found as a result of CPR, there may be larger needle punctures in the abdomen and in the lower legs (shins) of children. Large needles (trocars) may still be in place at the time of autopsy.

Deaths in the Hospital Following Trauma: After near fatal injuries or sudden illnesses, the patient may survive the initial insult to the body, and even appear to be recovering, but then dies suddenly due to a complication or unforeseen event. These complications are to be considered mechanisms of death. *The underlying cause of death is the disease or injury that landed the patient in the hospital originally.* The following are common complications or unforeseen events that result in death following trauma and natural diseases.

Arrhythmias: Abnormal heart rhythms are common after stress from trauma or after a heart attack, particularly in older individuals with underlying heart disease. Loss of blood, electrolyte imbalances, and surgery can cause arrhythmias to occur more frequently. A patient with preexisting hypertension can have an enlarged heart (hypertensive heart disease) that is more sensitive to arrhythmias. Arrhythmias are treatable but can be fatal despite aggressive treatment.

Infections: Infections are difficult to prevent in trauma victims. For example, if the skin is broken, or the patient aspirates gastric contents while unconscious, an infection is expected to develop, so antibiotic treatment is started immediately. Victims of trauma, particularly those on a ventilator for a prolonged period of time, often get pneumonia despite rigorous treatment. Sepsis (infection of the blood) can develop in these patients as well, which can lead to shock (vascular collapse) and death. Because these infections are acquired in the hospital, the patient can have an infection with a bacterium that shows antibiotic resistance, such as MRSA (methicillin-resistant *Staphylococcus aureus*)

Electrolyte abnormalities and other blood chemistry abnormalities: Electrolytes include sodium, potassium, and calcium, to name a few. For example, very high or low potassium can contribute to cardiac arrest by causing arrhythmias. Trauma patients and other very ill patients can have serious changes in the delicate electrolyte balance due to blood loss and the shifting of fluids in the body. The kidneys can fail in these patients, further throwing off the electrolyte balance and causing the need for kidney dialysis to help replace the function of the kidneys. Another blood chemistry problem is acidosis from lack of oxygen to the tissues and lack of oxygen.

Rupturing of blood vessels and hemorrhage: During trauma, blood vessels can be damaged slightly and then spontaneously rupture at a later date. Blood vessels, particularly those that were severely damaged, can also rupture subsequently. Patients with preexisting aneurysms (ballooning and other defects) are at risk for blood vessel rupture during the stress of severe illness or trauma. Heparin and other "blood thinners" increase the risk of spontaneous rupture of blood vessels.

Blood clots (emboli or thromboemboli): Victims of trauma and virtually anyone confined to a bed or who is immobile is at high risk for thromboemboli. Most doctors and hospitals give different drugs and therapies to prevent the formation of thromboemboli. These therapies include coumadin and heparin, as well as special leg compression devices to stop clot formation. Nonetheless, clot formation can still occur. Approximately 95% of the time, blood clots form in the veins of the lower legs. Death occurs when large clots (pulmonary thromboemboli) break loose, travel up the veins of the legs, and go through the heart, plugging up the major blood vessels (pulmonary arteries) feeding the lungs. Less commonly, clots can form on the heart valves and travel to the brain, causing stroke and death.

Shock: Shock occurs when blood vessels are no longer able to maintain normal blood pressure and organs die because they are not perfused with blood that carries oxygen.

Disseminated intravascular coagulation (DIC): DIC occurs when the body is no longer able to clot blood normally. The smaller blood vessels begin to leak and the person dies of shock.

families that request an autopsy. The family can obtain a private autopsy by engaging a pathologist to perform the examination, usually at a fee.

Death Investigations Requiring an Autopsy

Autopsies are usually not required when the patient has been under the regular treatment of a physician for a potential terminal illness, and in such cases the treating physician can certify the death. However, when a person dies suddenly, unexpectedly, or under suspicious circumstances, even while under the documented treatment of a physician, an autopsy is usually required. Listed below are cases that usually require an autopsy. As one can see, virtually any death can meet the criteria for an autopsy.

Cases that Usually Require an Autopsy

Cases that usually require an autopsy include the following:

- Homicides
- Suicides
- Accidents that occur on the job
- Drivers in single-car accidents (could be a suicide or natural death)
- Sudden and unexpected deaths of children
- Deaths of pilots in aircraft crashes
- Natural deaths that might impact the community (e.g., meningitis)
- Fire deaths
- Accidental deaths caused by the negligence or reckless behavior of others
- Deaths of persons in custody of the state or other agency
- Accidents that occur without a witness
- Accidents in which natural disease is a factor
- Sudden, unexpected deaths of apparently healthy persons (usually younger than 75 years)
- Deaths in which the manner of death is not readily apparent
- Deaths in which litigation is reasonably expected
- Hospital deaths in which the quality of care is an issue
- All suspicious deaths

In all manners of death, there are cases that require an autopsy. While it would be easier to simply have a policy that would include autopsies in all deaths, this policy would be expensive, impractical, and a waste of resources. Not performing autopsies in some cases can cause problems at a later date, when further information might be needed for a legal proceeding or an insurance claim, for example. Having some guidelines is helpful, particularly in natural and accidental deaths where it can be unclear whether an autopsy is needed. If performing an autopsy is seriously considered in a death investigation, then one should be performed, in the author's experience; that is, "If you think about it, you should do it." The service to the public and the reputation of the MEC office is too important to save a few dollars for an inadequate investigation.

Natural Deaths

When a disease, a syndrome, or a combination of diseases is the primary cause of death, the manner of death is categorized as "natural." Investigating natural death is significant to the MEC for a number of reasons. Infectious diseases (such as meningitis), human immune deficiency virus (HIV), or hepatitis can be discovered and those who had contact with the deceased can be evaluated and treated. Inherited diseases can be diagnosed, saving current living and future descendants of the deceased from correctable medical conditions.

"Natural" is the most common manner of death. Apparent accidental deaths are often natural deaths — for example, the driver of a vehicle who suddenly swerves off the road and is found dead after only a minor crash. Myocardial infarction is a common cause of death in this situation. Finding natural disease by autopsy in this situation is important for a number of reasons. The cause of the automobile crash is known for accident reconstruction purposes. Life insurance policies often pay double indemnity if the manner of death is "accident." The use of alcohol and substance abuse is ruled out as a cause of the crash. In the investigation of sudden, unexpected death, most individuals also are found to have died of natural causes, usually cardiac in nature.

Some deaths, like cirrhosis of the liver, are classified as natural, even if the cause is chronic alcoholism. Although the person willingly drinks alcohol, and if he knows cirrhosis can result, the death is classified "natural." This classification is done both by convention and presumably because the alcohol-induced cirrhosis develops over 10, 20, or more years. If a smoker with severe emphysema continues to smoke and dies from respiratory failure, this death would also be classified "natural." If a person took arsenic chronically, for example, that death would be classified a "suicide."

Victims of homicides also have natural diseases. These diseases can accelerate death in some cases. In fact, an elderly man with severe heart disease might not survive the same gunshot wound a young, healthy person would survive. Blood loss from a leg wound, for example, would be easily tolerated by a healthy, young 20-year-old. The elderly man with cardiac disease might not survive the stress on the cardiovascular system, and develop a myocardial infarction. Because "we take the victim as we find him," we treat the elderly man's and the younger man's cases equally, and the manner of death is "homicide" in both cases. We do not blame or hold the victim accountable for his existing cardiovascular disease. The gunshot wound set into motion a chain of events resulting in death. Although the cardiac disease contributed to the death, the cause of death remains the gunshot wound.

Unnatural Deaths

An autopsy is necessary in most unnatural deaths, including homicides, suicides, accidents, and those deaths in which the manner of death cannot be classified with the available information (often termed "undetermined," "unclassified," or "could not be determined"). Unnatural death is not a manner of death, per se. In unnatural deaths, although the causes and manners of death might appear obvious at the scene, an autopsy is usually performed. In accidents, finding the cause of the accident is essential, and an autopsy is often a large part of that investigation. In apparent suicides, intent to kill oneself must be demonstrated. In homicides, evidence must be collected and injuries must be documented. An autopsy should *always* be performed in homicides or apparent homicides.

Homicides

Homicide is a medical-legal term and is defined as the killing of another human being, either by commission or omission. Murder, manslaughter, and reckless homicide are strictly legal terms referring to the degree of action in the homicide. Certifying a case "Manner of Death, Homicide" does not mean that the perpetrator committed murder, or will even face legal charges. The policeman shooting the school sniper is an example of "justifiable" homicide. Shootings and stabbings are the obvious homicides. A common question is, "Why, in the case of a witnessed homicide of a single gunshot wound of the head, is an autopsy necessary?" Here are but a few reasons for an autopsy in such a case:

- To confirm the cause and manner of death; that which is "obviously" true to a layperson's observation, occasionally proves to be false by examination of an expert
- To provide photographic evidence for court proceedings
- To obtain the bullet and match it to a purported gun
- To track a bullet through the body (e.g., the bullet might not have entered the brain, and the person was strangled instead by a second perpetrator)
- To obtain trace evidence
- Witnesses might die or change statements; therefore, independent confirmation of statements is needed
- To obtain specimens from the deceased for toxicology studies
- To gather medical data for expert medical testimony

- The forensic pathologist is a witness for the deceased; direct examination by the forensic pathologist allows him or her to explain direct observations, such as injuries, to the court
- To correlate the injuries and other observations on the body and the evidence with witness statements
- To generate a report for the defense and its experts to review
- Because the court and the jury have the expectation that such an exam should take place (i.e., doing a complete autopsy in homicides is a legal and medical standard in the United States)

For the above reasons and more, it is the duty of the forensic pathologist to conduct a full medical-legal autopsy so that no reasonable investigative question remains unanswered. A thorough job must be done even though the cause of death might seem obvious.

Suicides

Suicide is the independent, willful taking of one's own life. Suicides usually require an autopsy. Although rare, a common reason is to rule out a homicide that has been made to look like a suicide. Often because of movies, television, and books using this theme, friends and relatives can carry this notion, and it may appear as a real explanation to them. The suicide of a loved one can be a devastating and very emotional event for family and friends. These well-meaning people can cling to alternative theories to explain the death, such as homicide or an unusual accident. The religious implications of suicide are so powerful in some faiths that families might never agree with the ruling of suicide. Families and friends have been known to remove important evidence from the scene, presumably to prevent the conclusion that the death is a suicide.

A common theme in all suicides is the intent to kill oneself. Demonstrating this intent can be difficult. Scene investigation involves looking for evidence of this intent. For example, constructing a rope for hanging, wiring the trigger of a gun, and leaving a suicide note are common forms of evidence of intent.

Accidents

Accidents more often than not require an autopsy. Fatal accidents that happen on the job should have a full investigation, including an autopsy. Deaths at the workplace are usually investigated by the Occupational Safety and Health Administration (OSHA). Insurance companies might require an autopsy before paying benefits. In law enforcement deaths while on duty, an autopsy is an absolute requirement for the investigation and for the family to receive death benefits. Accidents involving alcohol or drugs have criminal implications and should receive a full investigation, including an autopsy.

Accidents that come from negligence should be investigated as well because these cases may end up in the criminal courts.

Occasionally, accidents can appear to be suicides — for example, in auto-erotic asphyxia. In this accidental form of death, the victim uses a ligature to enhance sexual activities. The ligature compresses the jugular veins, stopping venous return to the heart, and cutting off oxygen to the brain. If the victim slips or becomes unconscious, death can ensue within minutes, due to asphyxia. Also, intoxicated people can ingest an overdose or a lethal combination of drugs, accidentally. Ultimately, in some cases it can be difficult to determine if the intent of the person was suicide.

The Autopsy: Assembling a Puzzle

The essence of the autopsy is about working backward from one undeniable fact: that a death has occurred. Forensic pathologists look back in time to the point in the past when a disease or injury set into motion a chain of events that were ultimately, and tragically, fatal. An old axiom in forensic pathology is that "one takes the victim as one finds him." This simply means that the pathologist starts at the beginning of the death investigation, with a deceased victim, and makes no other assumptions. Facts are determined as the result of the examination of this specific victim, with his or her unique set of circumstances, medical conditions, and injuries.

Forensic pathologists do not work in a vacuum, however. Information is collected from various sources, including interacting with crime scene investigators, law enforcement, reviewing statements of witnesses, examination of the scene, and following those leads that the scene provides. Analysis of this information sets the foundation for the autopsy procedure, and the final opinions of the pathologist, including the cause and manner of death.

A comprehensive medical-legal autopsy has three phases:

1. *Premorgue analysis.* Premorgue analysis is knowledge of the death scene, witness statements, environmental conditions at the scene, and the known circumstances surrounding the death. The pathologist often relies on the DSI for this information.
2. *Morgue analysis, or the autopsy, per se.* This phase includes external (including photography and collecting trace evidence) and internal examination of the body.
3. *Postmorgue analysis.* This phase occurs over the ensuing weeks to months and includes analysis of microscopic slides of tissues sampled during the autopsy procedure. Toxicologic, microbiologic culture, chemical, and other laboratory results are reviewed in this phase also. Special forensic tests such as DNA identification are assimilated as well. Often, additional

investigative information is received during this time period.The facts obtained from all three phases of analysis are assembled like the pieces of a puzzle to form a picture or snapshot of the person just before death. The forensic pathologist views this picture or puzzle of assembled facts to render an opinion, most importantly the cause and manner of death. The pertinent assembled facts and opinions are included in a written autopsy report. Occasionally, pieces of the puzzle are missing. In such cases, the forensic pathologist must use his or her experience and training to fill in the missing pieces to render an opinion.

Because opinion is formed by the facts at hand, if the facts change, so can the opinion. For example, initially a gross autopsy in a case of sudden, unexpected death, might show severe coronary disease. Days later when the toxicology analysis is reported, and high levels of multiple drugs are found, the cause of death must be changed to "multiple drug toxicity." Thus, the opinion given by the pathologist is only based on the facts that are known to him or her. If the facts are insufficient, the pathologist may have "no opinion," and the cause and manner of death ruled undetermined.

External Examination of the Body

Suiting Up: Universal Precautions

Protection of the pathologist, autopsy assistants, investigators, and medical personnel at the autopsy is not only a good idea; it is required by OSHA regulations. This protection is called universal precautions. To perform an autopsy, the pathologist and the assistant wear hats, masks, gowns, shoe covers, mesh gloves, and latex gloves (Figure 11.1). Some facilities use vacuum-assisted saws to gather bone dust from skull and rib sawing. All cases are treated as potentially infectious from blood-borne pathogens. While pathologists handle with care those cases known to be infectious, one must not be casual about the routine case that can harbor a latent hepatitis or HIV, for example. This is the reason all cases are treated as potentially infectious.

Opening the Body Bag

Once everyone is properly suited up for blood-borne pathogen protection, the body bag can be opened. Identification tags are placed on the body and the bag at the scene. Tags placed on the outside of the bags can become lost, so tagging the body directly is essential as well. The body is placed in a clean plastic body bag (Figure 11.2). Some pathologists recommend that the body be wrapped in a clean white sheet, because trace evidence can be lost in the large body bag. This sheet is carefully examined at the autopsy.

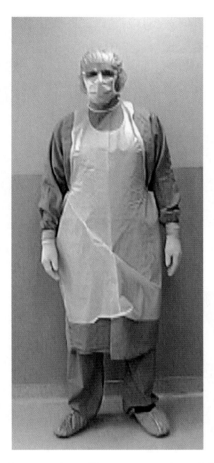

Figure 11.1 Universal precautions. Proper protection of the pathologist and all assistants against infectious diseases is essential. Eye protection, mouth and nose protection, double and cut-resistant gloves, waterproof barrier, and long-sleeve gown keep potential infectious agents away from the prosectors (those who cut) of the autopsy.

The hands are also bagged (preferably with paper bags) at the scene in suspicious deaths. Trace evidence has a higher chance of being on the hands, presumably because the victim grabs or contacts the victim in some way to transfer trace evidence, such as hair, skin, or grass as seen in the Figure 11.3. In practice, successful retrieval of useful trace evidence from the bagged hands is not very common. However, the one case of many that yields a DNA match or fiber match makes bagging the hands in every case worthwhile. Also, bagging the hands is usually expected by juries and the courts. Not bagging the hands can be used by defense attorneys to cast doubt on the thoroughness of the entire death investigation.

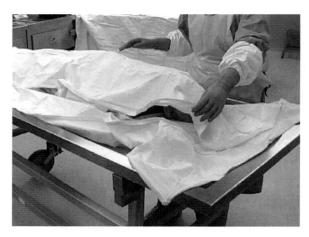

Figure 11.2 Opening the body bag. The body is placed in a clean white body bag. Some wrap the body in a clean white sheet to help contain potential trace evidence.

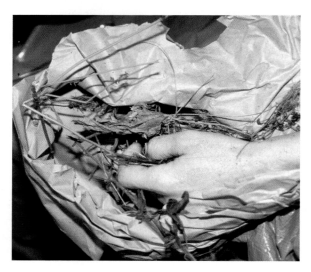

Figure 11.3 Trace evidence in bagged hands. The hands are bagged in all homicides. This allows more careful examination of trace evidence at the autopsy. This individual has a death grip on some trace evidence.

Clothing and Valuables

The clothing itself is evidence. Also, trace evidence might be on the clothing. For this, and practical reasons, the clothing is not removed at the scene. Trace evidence can easily be lost in the uncontrolled environment of the scene when removing the clothes. Rarely, an exception is made in cases where moisture can alter a substance or evidence on the clothing, because placing the body in the cooler can cause condensation in the bag.

The clothing can be quite helpful in death investigation because it is intimately associated with the body. A common example is determining the range of fire in a gunshot wound from a shirt the victim was wearing when shot. Unburned particles from the weapon will tattoo the bare skin. If clothing intervenes between the weapon and the skin, the majority of the unburned particles form a pattern on the clothing, with very little material going through the clothing to the skin. (Figure 11.4) This clothing can be analyzed by a forensic scientist to estimate the range of fire of the weapon, the width and configuration correlating to the distance of the shirt from the weapon. With rare exception, clothing should not be altered, removed, or cut at the scene. Clothing should not be cut in a homicide case. Clothing can contain unusual evidence, and therefore should be carefully removed.

Since we place the life of an individual above all else, clothing is often cut, otherwise altered, or removed at the scene of a violent death by first responders, such as paramedics. Removing the clothing is part of the routine examination of the patient, especially a victim of trauma. If the body is removed from the scene and taken to the hospital, the body is often fully undressed, possibly irreversibly altering, losing, or contaminating any trace evidence. Hospital personnel must save the clothing so that the death investigation agency can retrieve it. Even cut, removed clothing can be valuable, in determining gun shot distance, for example. The first responders to the medical emergency must be careful not to destroy evidence when any suspicion of violent death or injury exists. Obvious bullet holes or other significant evidence on clothing should not be cut or altered if possible.

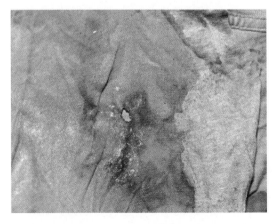

Figure 11.4 Gunshot of a shirt. The presence of an intervening object, such as clothing, between the gun barrel and skin can alter the soot pattern on the skin. Dark soot can be seen on and around the gunshot hole. Although it is *not* the duty of the forensic pathologist to issue a report on clothing examination, the clothing should be surveyed to better understand the wound on the body.

Body Storage

The body must be stored in a secure cooler at about 37°F, preferably under lock and key (Figure 11.5). Only a limited number of individuals should have the key. A complete log sheet of arrival times and all encounters with the body should be maintained indefinitely. This log should include all valuables. Any personal item that is not evidence should be logged, described, and retained for the family. Items that appear not to have value to the investigator might have value to the family, so care and consideration of these items is recommended. The trinket that was once cheap becomes expensive jewelry once lost. Valuables can become evidence. This watch shown in Figure 11.6 was broken during an attack with a golf club. It was thought to have been broken at the exact time of the assault, a rarity in practice.

Trace Evidence

Trace evidence for the purpose of the autopsy are those substances, materials, or objects, visible or invisible, that are present on, in, or around the body, which potentially have value as evidence. Obvious trace evidence that might be lost in transport can be collected at the scene. Common objects collected at the scene include hair or small fibers or paint flakes that could

Figure 11.5 Lockable cooler. Bodies should be kept in a lockable cooler, with a registry of all valuables being kept. All activity in and out of the cooler should be logged. Cooler temperature is kept between about 37 and 45°F.

Figure 11.6 Broken watch. Valuables can become evidence, such as this watch that was broken during an assault. The victim (and the watch) received many blunt force injuries, a few of which were from a golf club.

be easily lost. Because scene lighting is often poor and the setting inappropriate, any further taking of trace evidence is best taken in the autopsy suite (Figure 11.7). One method for preparing the body for transport is to place a clean sheet over the body and then place it in a clean body bag.

Focus on What Is Not Obvious

The external examination of the deceased is a focused head-to-toe examination of the body. This exam is similar to a physical exam one might get from his physician.

All parts of the body are examined, from the hair on top of the head to the toenails. The pathologist spends as much time on the external exam as he or she does on the internal exam. The pathologist is always looking for trace evidence on the skin, clothing, in wounds, or in orifices of the body. The tendency is to focus on the obvious gunshot wound or gaping laceration. The pathologist focuses on the other areas of the body first, then finally on the obvious injury. Most pathologists have a systematic examination process designed to carefully survey all systems, being careful not to overlook any area of the body (Figure 11.8).

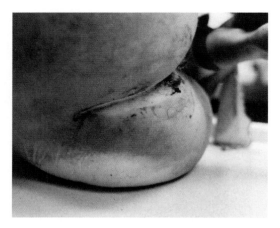

Figure 11.7 Trace evidence on the buttocks. In sexual assaults, trace evidence might be as fine as a single hair, as seen on the buttock here. This small, fine evidence can be lost on the transfer of the body, and is one exception to taking evidence from the body at the scene. Pubic hair from the body can be analyzed with the suspect's, such as was done in this case, producing an identification match.

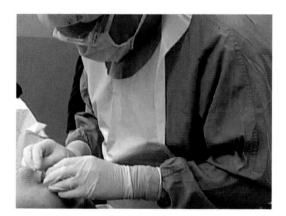

Figure 11.8 Examination of the mouth. The pathologist must perform a detailed systemic exam of the entire body, being careful not to overlook any body system. During the external exam, the focus is taken off the obvious injury.

When examining an organ, tissue, or region of the body, the pathologist looks for:

- Traumatic injuries, both old and new
- Natural disease processes, such as tumors or atherosclerosis
- Congenital defects or deformities
- Toxicologic, thermal (burns), and chemical injuries
- Trace evidence

- Infectious disease processes
- Anything abnormal, unusual, or unexpected: excepting chance, one does find something he does not look for

Documenting Traumatic Injuries

Diagrams and Descriptions

Documenting injuries is one of the principal goals of the forensic autopsy. The body is assessed from head to toe. The injury is examined from the outside of the body to the inside. The injuries are photographed, measured, diagrammed, and described. The autopsy records must accurately depict these injuries, both in a written, descriptive manner and in a visual form. Diagrams and sketches are generally used for note taking. Any diagrams made during the autopsy are incorporated into the autopsy report and should not be interpreted independent of the autopsy report.

Because most pathologists are not artists, and it is virtually impossible to draw an adequate diagram, photography is the professional standard in documenting significant injuries (Figure 11.9). It is essential that the significant injuries are well documented, both by descriptions in the report and by photography. In the court system, another expert will undoubtedly be involved. It is the ethical duty of the forensic pathologist to provide accurate documentation of his or her observations. Failure to document can cause potential difficulties in court, because defendants are legally allowed to examine the evidence against them.

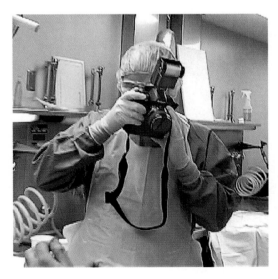

Figure 11.9 Documentation by photography. Photography of injuries is an essential part of the autopsy.

Radiology and Imaging

In the autopsy suite, radiographs are primarily used in routine cases:

- *To evaluate gunshot wounds,* to locate and enumerate bullets, bullet fragments, and other metallic objects.
- *To evaluate stab wounds or puncture wounds.* Occasionally, a portion of a knife, scissor, or other sharp metallic object will break off when it strikes bone.
- *For identification.* Jaw radiographs are used to compare with dental records of the purported victim. Unique metallic implants, such as rods in the back, can aid identification.
- *To evaluate child or elder abuse,* to find subtle or healed fractures.
- *To evaluate unusual deaths,* such as explosions or plane crashes.
- *To examine severely charred or decomposed remains* for hidden objects (e.g., bullets) or identification.
- *To document characteristic fractures,* such as the so-called nightstick fracture of the forearm, classically a blunt force injury sustained by the victim holding his arm up to block a nightstick attack (Figure 11.10).

The autopsy is much more sensitive in finding fractures of certain areas, such as the skull, ribs, or hyoid bone, because the bone is directly visualized. Hemorrhage resulting from the fracture enhances the visibility of the fracture (Figure 11.11). The radiograph is simply a tool to supplement the autopsy. There are many more uses for radiographs and other

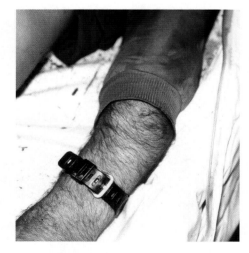

Figure 11.10 Forearm fracture. External exam of this forearm reveals a somewhat obvious deformity. The question is: Was this bone fractured before or after death?

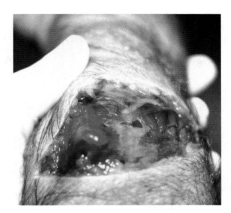

Figure 11.11 Incision of left forearm fracture (see Figure 11.10). Incision into the fracture reveals acute hemorrhage. This confirms that the fracture was premortem. Viewing fractures directly at autopsy, especially in the skull, is more sensitive than x-rays. It is not customary to cut the face, neck, or arms for an autopsy unless absolutely necessary.

imaging in forensic pathology; see Dix (1999) and Wagner (2004) for further information.

Photography and Video as Documentation Tools

As discussed above, in addition to providing a detailed written report describing the findings, the pathologist must document pertinent injuries in cases of medical-legal significance. Photographs are the main visual documentation tool as a "true and accurate representation" of what the pathologist observed. Many states now have laws restricting who can view autopsy photographs. One should consult the laws in one's own jurisdiction to prevent improper viewing or release of autopsy photographs.

In homicide cases, pictures are taken of nearly every step of the autopsy, from opening the bag, to documenting the final injury. Injuries are photographed both before and after the wounds are cleaned. It is crucial to clean the wounds, removing blood or debris. Only then can the true configurations of the wounds be revealed (Figure 11.12a,b). Also, the wound must be clearly demonstrated for another pathologist/expert to review. One must remember that the courtroom jury will likely view the photographs. A key job of the pathologist is to explain injuries to the Jury. Pictures that display the injury poorly do not aid in communication to the jury. Bloody, unclear, or unnecessarily grotesque photographs will probably not be admitted into evidence by the court.

Video is very useful when there are many, or complex injuries. In the author's experience, videotaping the entire autopsy, however, is not a useful tool.

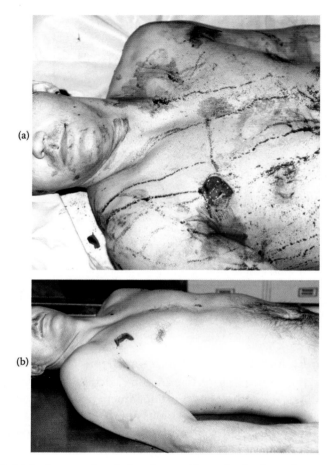

Figure 11.12 (a) Stab wounds of the chest. When the body is first examined, blood covers the injuries. Blood spatter and drainage patterns are important to document and study, so these are photographed. After this, the body must be cleaned so the wounds can be studied. (b) Stab wounds of chest after washing away the blood (see Figure 11.12a). The stab wound configurations can be seen clearly now that the blood has been cleaned away from the chest and trunk.

External Examination

Specific Body Areas

Overall "Gestalt"

After the body has been undressed and carefully cleaned, the pathologist steps back from the body and looks at the overall position or shape of the body (habitus). Is the body symmetrical? Is there morbid obesity, or is the frame extremely thin (cachexia)? Is there an overall deformity? For example, is the body in a fetal position? Is there something amiss, or out of place? This is also a good time for the pathologist to reflect on what has been done to this point, and what is about to be done.

Skin

The skin is technically an organ, per se. It is the organ that is most carefully assessed on the external examination. The skin acts as an outward sentinel, or red flag, for deep injuries or diseases within the body. The skin of the individual in Figure 11.13a shows a brown pigmentation on the trunk. Multiple brown, greasy appearing benign moles are seen, known as seborrheic keratoses. Seeing this number of lesions alerts the pathologist to look for an internal cancer, usually of the gastrointestinal tract. In fact, in this case, this unfortunate individual had carcinoma of the colon (Figure 11.13b).

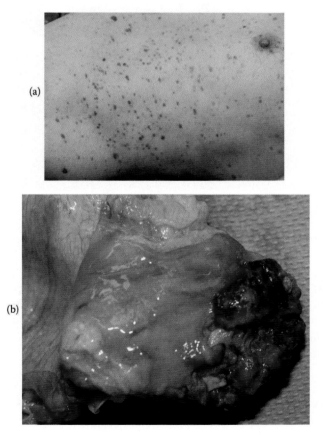

Figure 11.13 Acanthosis nigricans, seborrheic keratoses, and carcinoma of the colon. (a) Dark pigmentation of the skin and multiple "greasy" keratoses on the body alert the pathologist to look internally for a visceral cancer. (b) In the rectal-sigmoid colon of this patient, a carcinoma was found.

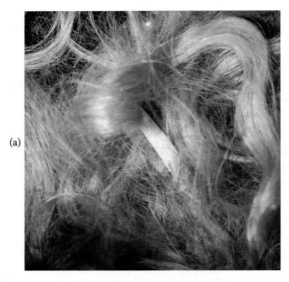

(a)

(b)

Figure 11.14 (a) Broken knife found in the hair. The hair must be carefully examined for evidence. (b) The murder weapon was found in the hair of this victim, a broken kitchen knife.

Hair

Hair color is noted for identification. Hair roots can be used for DNA identification. At least 100 hairs must be pulled, not cut. Hair can contain trace evidence or gross evidence, such as the knife that was used to murder the individual in Figure 11.14a,b. Toxicologic analysis of hair is useful for diagnosing chronic drug use or poisoning.

Scalp

An injury to the scalp is often the sentinel to deeper injuries, like skull fractures, brain contusions, and hematomas. Hair can cover injuries, particularly those that do not bleed, so a careful examination must be undertaken. Small-caliber gunshot wounds are notoriously difficult to find in thick hair. Scalp injuries on the back of the head can be easily overlooked (Figure 11.15). To see a wound and photograph it properly, the hair around the wound is carefully

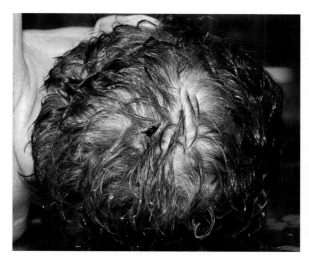

Figure 11.15 Laceration of the scalp. The blood has been washed out of the hair, exposing what appears to be a laceration. One cannot be sure until after shaving the hair around the wound and more closely examining the wound. (See also Figure 11.16.)

Figure 11.16 Close-up view of laceration of the scalp. The hair around the wound has been shaved, and the wound more carefully cleaned. One can see marginal abrasion, undermined margins, and tissue bridging. These findings, now clearly seen, demonstrate a laceration.

shaved (Figure 11.16). The wound in Figure 11.15 is a laceration with an abrasion of the margin. The skull below this area revealed a fracture in the back of the head, or occipital bone (Figure 11.17). The opposite part of the brain, or frontal lobe, shows contusions, indicating the person fell backward and was not struck in the head. This is a contracoup injury (Figure 11.18).

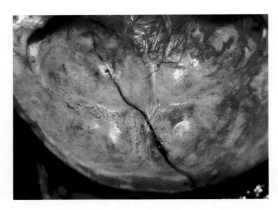

Figure 11.17 Fracture of occipital bone of the skull. This fracture was discovered below the laceration shown in Figures 11.15 and 11.16. One must conclude that this is a blunt force injury. The question remains: Was this person struck with a blunt force object, or was there a fall? (See also Figure 11.18.)

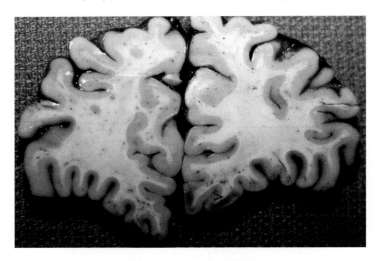

Figure 11.18 Contra-coup injury in the frontal lobe. Contusion hemorrhage can be seen at the arrows, near the bottom of the specimen. These contusions indicate a contra-coup contusion, meaning the victim fell backward, striking and fracturing the occipital bone. Because the brain is moveable inside the skull, the moving brain slaps against the frontal skull base, producing the contusions that are shown at the bottom of the figure by the arrows.

Face

The face is only dissected in rare cases — to retrieve a bullet or other evidence, for example. Every attempt should be made not to cut or alter the face, both out of respect for the individual and in consideration of viewing at the funeral services.

Facial injuries can be important in determining the driver when multiple individuals, usually unbelted, die in a motor vehicle crash. Identifying the driver

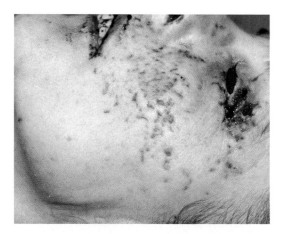

Figure 11.19 "Side glass" abrasions/lacerations. The face exam can be helpful in determining the driver in a motor vehicle crash. Because side glass is tempered, not laminated like windshield glass, it breaks up into small cubes, dicing the face. Although not absolute, injuries on the left side of the face might indicate the driver, and on the right side of the face, a passenger.

can be important if the vehicle was operated unlawfully (e.g., driving under the influence of alcohol). Side window glass is tempered, not laminated like the front windshield. Broken automotive side glass produces many small cubes that tend to cause small cubic cuts and abrasions on the face. Hence, the driver tends to have left face side glass injury. These conclusions, as always, do not prove driver or passenger and must be taken in context of the entire case (Figure 11.19).

Eyes

The eye (iris) color is recorded. The eyes are examined for hemorrhage. Small punctate (pointlike) hemorrhages in the conjunctiva (white part of the eye) often suggest an asphyxial cause of death (Figure 11.20). Yellow conjunctiva (jaundice) might indicate liver disease or hemolysis, a disorder of many different causes where the blood cells are broken apart in the body. The soft tissues around the eye (orbit) are very vascular. Blunt force to the area can easily cause contusion (a black eye), relative to many other areas of the body. Orbital soft tissue hemorrhage can also be seen in skull fractures involving the base of the frontal bone in particular (Figure 11.21). This point illustrates the aim of the external exam: the outward hemorrhage directs the pathologist to look inward for a cause.

Nose

The nasal cartilage can be fractured in traumatic injuries; therefore, palpation and increased range of motion can indicate fracture. Drug residues can be seen in the nares. The chronic snorting of drugs can damage the nasal mucosa.

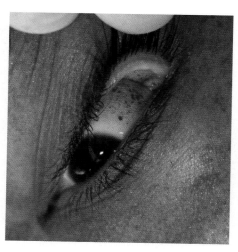

Figure 11.20 Conjunctival petechiae. Small pointlike hemorrhages in the conjunctiva, or clear membrane of the eye, are often seen in asphyxial deaths. These petechiae are due to the hemorrhage of small vessels in the conjunctiva, caused by the increased vascular pressure seen in asphyxia.

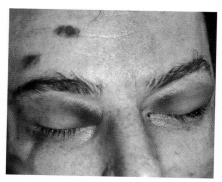

Figure 11.21 Orbital ecchymoses or "raccoon eyes." The darkening of the soft tissue around the eyes is due to blood accumulating in the soft tissues. This finding alerts the pathologist to search for fractures in the base of the skull, most likely the frontal bone, or orbital roofs.

Mouth

The mouth can be tightly clinched due to rigor mortis. In such cases, the mouth is difficult to open. Examination of the mouth after rigor is released is much easier. The teeth are examined, and visible teeth are cataloged. Unusual teeth or dental appliances can be used to make an identification. Dental caries (cavities) are noted. Drug residue can be seen, as in cases of drug abuse or overdose. In sexual assault cases, oral examination and swabs are taken to look for spermatozoa. In suffocation and strangulation cases, there are often injuries in the mouth (Figure 11.22). This particular injury can occur when the perpetrator forcibly holds the mouth closed.

Neck

The skin of the anterior neck is examined for contusions or abrasions, suggesting manual or ligature strangulation (Figure 11.23a). The thyroid gland is palpated in the lower lateral neck. The neck is manually examined for tumor masses and enlarged lymph nodes (Figure 11.23b). The range of motion of

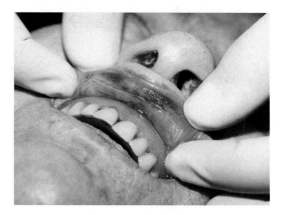

Figure 11.22 Examination of the mouth. The mouth and teeth are examined for injuries and foreign material. The mouth is difficult to open much in most autopsies because the jaw muscles are tightly clenched due to rigor mortis. The upper lip shows contusion and abrasion in a victim who was strangled and suffocated. This injury was produced by external pressure on the mouth.

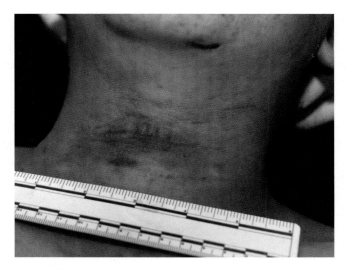

Figure 11.23 Neck abrasions and contusions in strangulation. Multiple abrasions and contusions of the anterior neck are usually seen in strangulation injury. Searching for internal injuries of this neck is essential to opine that these injuries are due to strangulation.

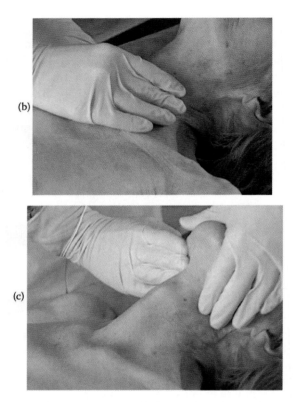

Figure 11.23 (b) and (c) Examination of the neck. The neck is palpated for masses, enlarged lymph nodes, and thyroid abnormalities. Tracheal deviation can indicate air in the chest or neck (pneumothorax and mediastinum).

the neck is checked. A highly flexible range of motion is abnormal because of rigor mortis, and reminds the pathologist to look for a fracture on internal examination.

Chest
The chest is examined for symmetry and size (Figure 11.24a). Patients with emphysema and other chronic diseases often have an expanded or "barrel" chest. Crepitus, or a crackling, feeling, indicates subcutaneous air from a pneumothorax. Rib fractures can be palpated as well. In severe chest injuries, such as from a high-speed motor vehicle crash, the chest can appear collapsed (Figure 11.24b).

Breasts
The skin and nipple are observed for masses and ulcerations. The breast is palpated for masses and tumors (Figure 11.25a). The axilla, or armpit, is examined for enlarged lymph nodes. Breast cancers commonly spread to these axillary lymph nodes (Figure 11.25b,c)

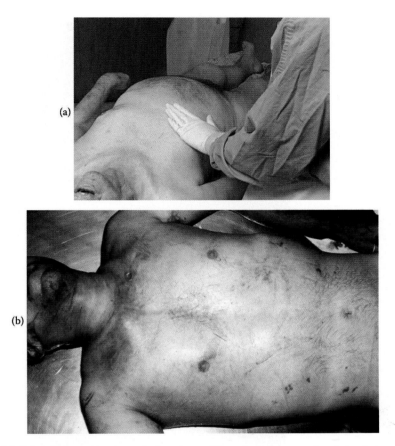

Figure 11.24 (a) Examination of the chest. The chest is examined for injures, such as rib fractures or crepitus due to air in the soft tissues. The chest in (b) is flattened due to fracture of all the ribs anteriorly. This was due to a high-speed crash, in excess of 100 mph, causing a failure of the airbag and a crushing of the chest wall.

Abdomen

The abdomen is visually examined for distention, or bloating. Victims who have had cardiopulmonary resuscitation often have distension in the epigastric area. This is a result of air going into the stomach. The abdomen can also become distended (Figure 11.26a) due to hemorrhage or ascites (Figure 11.26b). Ascites is the accumulation of fluid in the abdomen in conditions such as cirrhosis of the liver. Distension can also be seen due to bowel rupture and extensive inflammation, alerting the pathologist to take microbiologic cultures when opening the abdomen.

The abdomen is a common place for scars. The pathologist should search for scars, including gallbladder, appendectomy, and other surgical scars. The presence or absence of the scars can be used for making an identification.

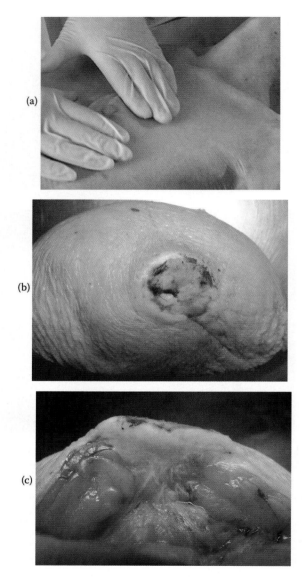

Figure 11.25 Breast exam and breast carcinoma. (a) The breasts are examined visually and by palpation for tumors and other deformities. (b and c) Surgical specimens showing a large, ulcerating tumor of the nipple. (c) The cut section demonstrates a white tumor in the midline infiltrating the surrounding fat.

Extremities, Hands, Fingers, and Nails

The pathologist must focus on the extremities, hands, fingers, and nails. These are areas easily forgotten, probably because examinations here rarely elicit the cause of death. These areas are often rich in trace evidence and in clues to the cause and manner of death. For example, the extremities bear the

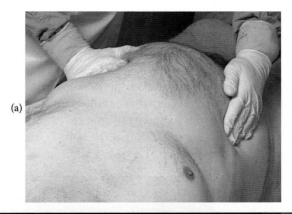

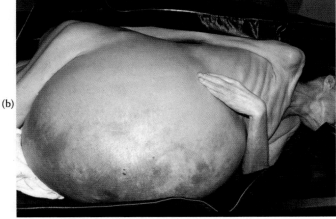

Figure 11.26 Abdominal examination. The abdomen is visually examined for distension and other abnormalities. Both (a) and (b) show distension, in (b), the extreme. The abdomen is palpated for solid masses and enlargement of the spleen and liver. In (b), the patient died from carcinoma of the ovary. The extremely distended abdomen is the result of excessive fluid in the abdominal cavity.

brunt of knife attacks. Victims often grab the knife and place their hands in a defensive position to ward off the attack (see Figure 11.27a). These wounds are often referred to as defense wounds. The hands, nails, and fingers can carry trace evidence from a weapon or a perpetrator, such as wood fragments, hair, and skin. For this reason, the hands are carefully examined and the fingernails are scraped. Careful examination can show a portion of a missing nail. The death scene can be searched for this torn nail fragment (Figure 11.27b).

Clues to natural disease processes can be seen in the hands and fingers. Splinter hemorrhages seen in the fingernail beds (Figure 11.27c) in this case were an external sign of the vegetation on the aortic valve of this patient, a condition called bacterial endocarditis. Bacterial-laden thrombi break off the valve and travel in the arterial system to the ends of the fingers, and more ominously, the brain, causing an abscess.

Back

Because bodies are not easily turned over, examination of the back can be overlooked. To prevent this, the back is examined ritualistically at the same point in every autopsy. The back is a large area covering the back of the chest and the back of the abdomen, and even the posterior portions of the neck and abdomen. If many or key injuries are seen, the body is carefully turned prone (face down) for documentation and examination of these injuries. Occasionally, while the anterior or front portion of the body is free of injuries, the back contains a serious injury (Figure 11.28).

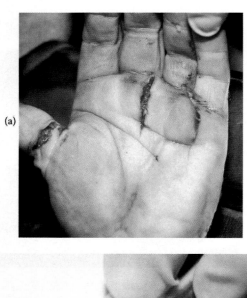

(a)

(b)

Figure 11.27 Examination of the hands and fingers. Examination of the hands is useful in both forensic and medical cases. The hands usually must be opened for examination because rigor mortis often causes them to be clenched. (a) Defense cuts on the palmar surface of the hand, wounds obtained defending a knife attack. (b) A finger and broken nail from a homicide victim. The broken nail was found at a second crime scene, where the victim was most likely assaulted. Finding and matching this missing nail implicated a suspect in this strangulation homicide.

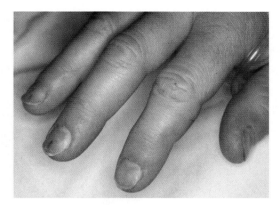

Figure 11.27(c) Splinter hemorrhages in the middle and ring finger nail beds. This is a sign of bacterial endocarditis and vegetations on the mitral or aortic heart valves. In this condition, small bacteria-laden emboli are disseminated throughout the arterial system into the nailbeds, kidneys, and brain.

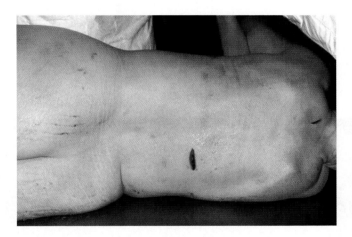

Figure 11.28 Stabs wounds found on examination of the back. Bodies are difficult to turn over, so there is a natural tendency to forget to look at the back. Autopsy protocols are designed so that the back exam is not overlooked, which in the case depicted one would miss at least two stab wounds.

Genitalia

Male genitalia are assessed for the presence or absence of circumcision. This observation can be helpful in identification. The testes are assessed for tumors. Rarely, an undescended testis is noted. Injuries, such as abrasions or bite marks, can be seen in a sexual assault. If the penis has been traumatically severed, the resultant blood loss can be fatal.

The female genitalia are examined for tumors, or developmental anomalies. In unnatural deaths, the female genitalia are examined for injury from sexual assault. This includes an entire sexual assault protocol, including an initial external examination for trace evidence such as hair. The vaginal area and rectum are examined for injuries (Figure 11.29a). The vagina, rectum, and surrounding areas are swabbed for semen or other secretions. Hair and other trace evidence is sought. The underpants and clothing are collected. The author

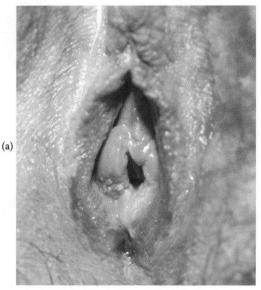

Figure 11.29 Abrasions on vaginal examination. Examination for sexual assault is essential in suspicious death. Excessive abrasion, laceration, or contusion of the genitalia usually indicates assault. (a) The labia here show a great deal of abrasion. (b) A full sexual assault kit was obtained during this case, confirming the assault. The victim was strangled to death during the assault.

has found commercially available sexual assault kits convenient because they contain more than enough material to do the examination (Figure 11.29b).

Rectum/Anus

The anus is examined, as above, in both sexes for sexual assault. Tumors and ulcerations are common findings in this region. In the bedridden, the sacral region, buttocks, and lateral ankles should be examined for pressure sores. The presence of such injuries might indicate elder abuse. Inflammatory bowel diseases, such as Crohn's disease, can be seen from the anus (Figure 11.30).

Internal Examination

Opening of Body Cavities and Initial Assessment

As has been shown, the external exam provides clues that give us leads about what we can expect to find inside the body. The internal exam is where these leads are investigated. As with any investigation, some findings are totally unexpected. This means the pathologist must examine all the tissues carefully and objectively. Going into an autopsy with a preconceived notion about what the findings will be can cause the pathologist to overlook unexpected findings. For this reason, each internal exam includes, at the minimum, examination of the:

- Heart, including coronary arteries and heart valves
- Chest cavity and mediastinum
- Lungs and lung hilum

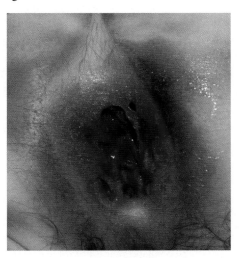

Figure 11.30 Inflammatory bowel disease on anal examination. The anus is examined for assault as well as medical conditions. The injury depicted shows multiple ulcerations and fistulae, caused by inflammatory bowel disease, most likely Crohn's disease. Inflammatory bowel disease causes ulcerations in the bowel wall and mucosa. If untreated, this disease can cause peritonitis and death.

- Liver and gallbladder
- Spleen
- Stomach and esophagus
- Small and large intestines
- Bowel mesentery
- Peritoneal cavity
- Body walls
- Aorta and its branches
- Kidneys and adrenal glands
- Bladder
- Prostate
- Uterus and ovaries
- Neck organs, including larynx and thyroid gland
- Vertebral column
- Skull
- The brain and its coverings

The above is a general list. Special cases or circumstances might require a more focused study in a given tissue or organ system.

During the internal exam, the pathologist is continuously looking for injuries and diseases with every cut of the knife. All the senses are used (except taste, of course). Tumors are often hard and can be palpated with the fingers. Hemorrhage can be seen in the tissues with deep traumatic contusions. A smell of bitter almonds might indicate cyanide poisoning. Hearing delicate crackles in the chest and mediastinal tissues indicates air in the tissues, or pneumothorax. The dissection is a careful, stepwise examination of the tissues and organs, usually done in the same way so that nothing is forgotten. Most pathologists use their own routine protocols for dissection for this reason.

One should follow the figures page-by-page (Figures 11.30 through 11.72) to experience the actual steps taken during the autopsy dissection.

Figure 11.31 Dissection of chest skin and soft tissue. The skin and subcutaneous tissue are dissected back to expose the underlying muscle and bone. The natural yellow color of the subcutaneous fat can be seen here.

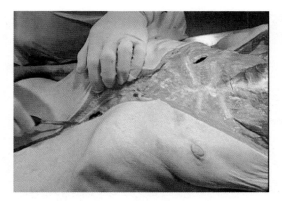

Figure 11.32 Opening of the abdominal cavity. The abdomen is opened, exposing the underlying viscera. The pathologist is constantly looking for fluid, hemorrhage, or signs of inflammation in the abdominal cavity.

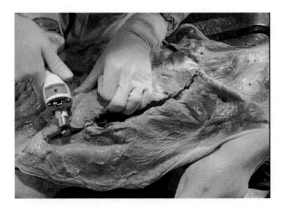

Figure 11.33 Opening of the ribs with a bone saw. The ribs are sawed and opened with wide arcs to facilitate access to the chest organs and tissues.

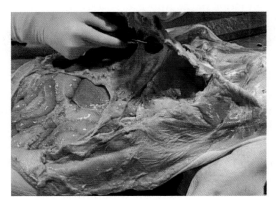

Figure 11.34 Removing the "chest plate." The anterior diaphragm, uncut soft tissue, and soft tissue of the mediastinum are dissected, as the "chest plate," or sternum and ribs, is lifted off.

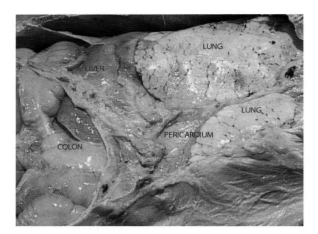

Figure 11.35 Survey of lungs. After the chest plate is removed, the lungs are examined *in situ*. The lungs here are situated normally in the chest.

Figure 11.36 Opening of the pericardium. The pericardium is opened, looking for fluid and inflammation of the lining (pericarditis).

Organ and Tissue Removal

In the Virchow autopsy method, the organs are removed one after another in an organized, logical fashion; for example, the neck organs are removed after the viscera are removed, to negate any artifact from congestion. Other organ removal methods include the Gohn, Letulle, or modified Rokitansky methods, where the organs are removed *en bloc* (all together). This allows the internal viscera to be examined while still being connected together. This method is always used by some pathologists. The author has found the Gohn method useful in infants with multiple cardiac and other birth defects. There is no right or wrong method of dissection; the aim is simply to perform a complete autopsy and to provide a detailed description of that autopsy.

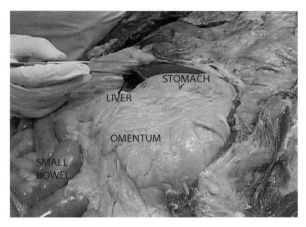

Figure 11.37 Upper abdominal organs. The liver is lifted up with the forceps as it rests on the stomach. The omentum (protective fat layer) is seen below the stomach, partially covering the bowel.

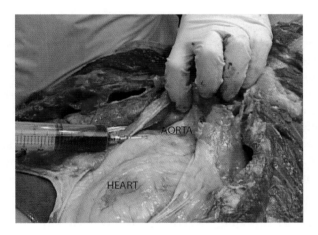

Figure 11.38 Taking blood from the aorta. Routinely, blood is removed from the aorta, or inferior vena cava. Blood is preferable when the concentration of a specific drug or toxin must be known (e.g., alcohol or carbon monoxide).

Individual Organ Exam

Each organ and tissue is generally examined from the outside to the inside, from observing the "gross" or macroscopic appearance, dissecting the organ, and then studying the microscopic features. The objectives are to:

- Examine and observe the diseases or injuries of each organ or tissue in a systematic, complete fashion.
- Make diagnoses and form opinions about the etiologies of the diseases or injuries. This is done by examining the gross organ on the day of the

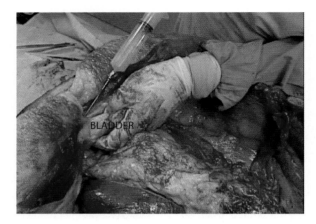

Figure 11.39 Removing urine from the bladder. At least 7 cc is preferable to screen for most drugs, toxins, and poisons. Urine is the preferable body fluid to screen for the drugs most commonly abused. For some drugs and toxins, tissues such as brain, muscle, fat, hair, liver, kidney, bone, and nails are preferable. For example, arsenic is best found in the hair and nails.

autopsy, and by looking at microscopic sections of the organ or tissues at a later date.

- Describe the disease, disorder, or injury and make a record of the observations. This allows other experts to review the report and draw independent conclusions about the data provided.
- Document pertinent diseases or injuries by photography or other media.
- Preserve pertinent tissues either in fixative or paraffin so that additional studies can be performed at a later date. For example, hemorrhagic soft tissue of the neck is often retained in strangulation cases.

Examination of the Head, Skull, Brain, and Spinal Cord

All medical-legal examinations require the examination of the head, skull, and brain. This includes careful examination of the scalp, skull, and dura mater, the fibrous membrane that tethers the brain in place. Because the brain is the supreme organ system, giving orders to the rest of the body, no examination is complete without assessing the brain and its coverings. At times, the question is raised, Why does the "head" need to be examined when the cause of death is obvious? Aside from the reasons given in Chapter 2 for doing an autopsy when the cause of death is "obvious," some additional reasons for examining the head include:

- The scalp and hair can hide contusions and other injuries. Examining the scalp from the bottom side can make these injures evident.
- Postmortem skull x-rays do not show small fractures.

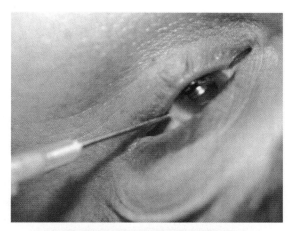

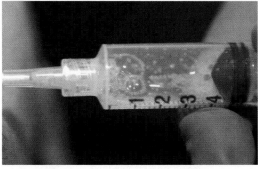

Figure 11.40 (a and b) Obtaining vitreous fluid from the eye. Vitreous humor, or clear liquid fluid in the eye, is obtained routinely. Because the vitreous fluid tends to concentrate drugs and other analytes, testing is useful in a number of cases. For example, blood glucose is not reliable post mortem. A very high postmortem vitreous glucose can aid in the diagnosis of diabetic hyperglycemia (high blood sugar).

- In the author's experience, CAT (computerized axial tomography) scans performed on the injured person can miss up to 10 cc of subdural blood.
- Unexpected tumors, old injuries, inflammation (e.g., meningitis), strokes, or other conditions are often found.
- A common injury seen in forensic pathology practice is the subdural hematoma. Often, the mechanism of sustaining a subdural hematoma is by falling on a hard surface. Small blood vessels between the dural layer and the brain (bridging vessels) are severed, causing bleeding and hematoma. The brain must be examined for this injury.

Microscopic Examination

Making diagnoses through the microscope is the tool and trade of most pathologists. If one has a breast biopsy, or a tumor removed, it is the pathologist who

Figure 11.41 Heart removal, cutting the inferior vena cava. The inferior vena cava is cut, as are the pulmonary veins, pulmonary arteries, and the aorta. The heart is held in the left hand in this figure. Blood flows from the cut vessels if the blood is not clotted, decomposed, or mostly absent from the body. In cases of severe hemorrhage, there is a notable absence of blood at this moment of the autopsy.

Figure 11.42 Excision of lungs. The lungs are removed at the hilum, or center of attachment.

classifies the tumor and diagnoses the lesion as benign or malignant. The skill of making microscopic diagnoses is very useful in postmortem exams because the microscopic exam is used to support the gross findings in an autopsy.

The gross examination portion of the autopsy yields the cause and manner of death most of the time. That is to say, the pathologist normally walks away from the autopsy suite with a good idea of the major diagnoses and the cause and manner of death. For example, the pathologist does not need to look at microscope slides to diagnose a contact gunshot wound of the head. However, he or she will take sections of the wound to confirm, microscopically, that there is heavy soot deposition in the wound. In much the same way, the microscopic exam serves, in most cases, to supplement the autopsy.

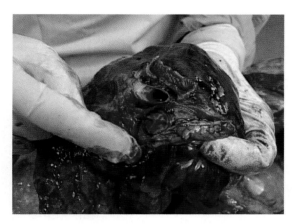

Figure 11.43 Examination of the hilum. As this right lung is removed, the hilum is quickly examined for tumor or infection. The lung is weighed. Heavy lungs are commonly seen in pneumonia and heart failure (associated with pulmonary edema).

There are cases where microscopic examination is pivotal in making a major diagnosis, and in determining the cause and manner of death. A partial list of these clinical situations include diagnosing:

- *Malignant tumors:* lung, colon, and breast carcinomas; lymphomas
- *Heart:* myocarditis, myocardial infarction
- *Lung:* pneumonia vs. congestion, often difficult to differentiate grossly
- *Liver:* chronic hepatitis
- *Spleen:* splenitis, one sign of sepsis
- *Kidneys:* nephridities, leading to renal failure (e.g., lupus)
- *Infections:* any tissue or organ. (e.g., meningitis or inflammation of the coverings of the brain)

Postmortem Laboratory Analysis

Drugs, Chemicals, and Poisons

The postmortem laboratory analysis of body fluids and tissues is an essential tool for the forensic pathologist. Toxicology studies are both useful in helping to determine the cause and manner of death and in answering key investigative questions. This book has shown the power of visual gross and microscopic findings in the autopsy. Drugs and chemicals, however, seldom leave characteristic or identifying visual findings at the autopsy. Even those substances that do leave visual findings [e.g., cyanide (pink livor) and carbon monoxide (red livor)] must be confirmed and quantified. The specific drugs or chemicals found, and their concentrations, tell us a story about the death. Discovering unexpected poisons can identify a perpetrator, or even save a life. For example, finding a blood carbon monoxide of 50% in a person who

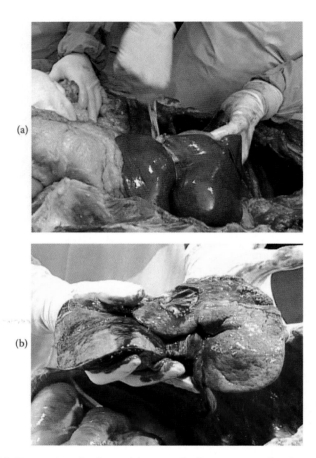

Figure 11.44 Removing the liver. (a) Once the liver is completely cut away, it is lifted out of the body for weighing. (b) Those who see the liver for the first time are astonished at its size and weight. The average liver weighs about 1930 grams, or about 4.5 pounds in a 170-pound man.

died at home during the winter might save the life of the other occupants by discovering a faulty furnace.

The pervasive use and abuse of alcohol, cocaine, marijuana, amphetamines, etc., and even prescription drugs in today's society necessitates the need to know whether or not these chemicals had any bearing on the death. The presence of these compounds is especially important if the death occurred on the job or as a result of a vehicle crash. Toxins and poisons in the environment, in the home, and in the workplace are increasingly common. OSHA will investigate deaths involving toxins or poisons in the workplace. Toxicology studies are required by the Federal Aviation Administration (FAA) and the National Transportation Safety Board (NTSB) in the investigation of many deaths, such as the pilot in airplane crashes.

Figure 11.45 Removing the spleen. The spleen is removed by cutting the vessels away from the hilum, checking carefully for lacerations because the capsule (covering) of the spleen can be easily torn on removal.

Figure 11.46 Bowel excision. In this removal method, the excision starts at the rectum and progresses upward toward the sigmoid colon in the left part of the abdomen.

Drug and alcohol analysis is part of a complete death investigation. To perform this analysis, the investigator, pathologist, and toxicologist must work together. The toxicologist heads up this team. Standard blood and urine screens are performed for commonly abused drugs and alcohol. These toxicology tests do not test for every possible drug or poison. If any drugs outside the standard screen are suspected, the toxicologist must be informed, because the method of analysis can depend on the compound suspected. In short, the investigator should say more to the toxicologist than simply, "Look for poison."

The Scene and the Body

The search for drugs and poisons begins at the death scene. Prescription drugs should be logged and the pills counted. One should be sure that the

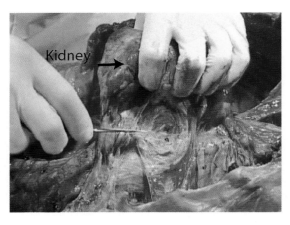

Figure 11.47 Removal of the kidney and ureter. The kidney is removed along with the ureter.

Figure 11.48 Opening the aorta. The aorta is opened from the iliac bifurcation upward to the ascending aorta.

drug in the container is the same as that on the label. Potentially fatal problems can arise when patients under therapeutic drug treatment by a physician take either less or more medication than prescribed. In accidental and suicidal overdoses, the number of pills present is much lower than should be present compared to the last refill date. Patients with a seizure disorder, for example, can succumb from *status epilepticus* (prolonged, violent seizure leading to respiratory arrest) if they stop taking prescribed seizure medication. The types of medication present speak to the medical history. The medication bottles list the prescribing physician, a good source of further information about the victim. Pertinent hospital, clinic, and doctors' office records should be reviewed.

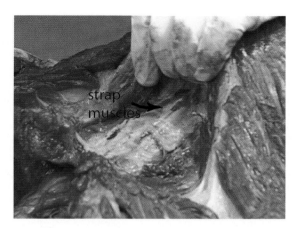

Figure 11.49 Neck dissection, exposing muscles. The neck is dissected after removing the viscera. While applying traction to the upper chest skin and soft tissue flap, the "strap" muscle group (midline) (shown here) and sternocleidomastoid (lateral) (shown in Figure 11.50) are revealed during careful dissection. The main focus of the dissection is to look for hemorrhage. If hemorrhage is discovered at any step, the dissection is photographed as it progresses. Suspected strangulation cases are imparted an even more detailed dissection than depicted here.

Figure 11.50 Neck dissection, exposing muscles. The neck is dissected after removing the viscera. While applying traction to the upper chest skin and soft tissue flap, the (a) "strap" muscle group (midline) (shown in Figure 11.49) and sternocleidomastoid (lateral) (shown here) are revealed during careful dissection. The main focus of the dissection is to look for hemorrhage. If hemorrhage is discovered at any step, the dissection is photographed as it progresses. Suspected strangulation cases are imparted an even more detailed dissection than depicted here.

Alcohol is the most common drug found in medical examiners' cases. Searching the death scene for empty alcohol containers and counting these containers is the first step. In addition to searching for illicit drugs, the trappings of drug abuse, such as paraphernalia, known "drug house," etc.,

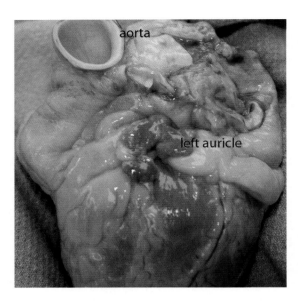

Figure 11.51 Anterior view of the heart. The normal heart is viewed after removal, showing the open aorta and smaller auricle or "ear" of the left atrium.

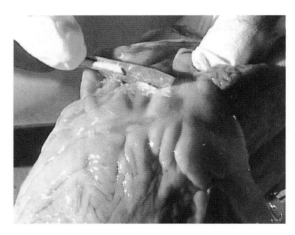

Figure 11.52 Cutting the left anterior descending coronary artery. A series of cuts is made along the entire length of the left anterior descending branch of the left coronary artery, usually the largest coronary artery of the heart. The artery must be examined from its origin, called the coronary ostium, so as not to overlook a focal thrombus or coronary disease.

should be noted. Often, drugs, needles, and the like can be found around or even on the body. In illicit drug deaths, witnesses commonly remove or dispose of the drugs. Searching arrest records can be helpful in discovering a drug abuse history. Drug-oriented tattoos, clothing, and other materials can alert the investigation team as well.

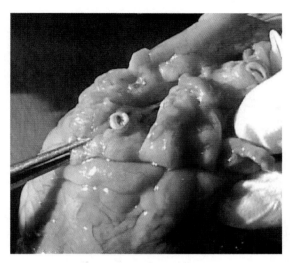

Figure 11.53 Left coronary artery thrombosis. This cut of the left main coronary artery shows nearly completely occlusive atherosclerosis. A small, dark thrombus occludes the lumen (seen near the tip of the forceps). Occlusion of the artery results in loss of blood flow to the region of the left ventricle of the heart that the artery supplies. Lack of blood flow results in a lack of oxygen (hypoxia) to the tissues. If the thrombus or blocking plaque continues to occlude the vessel wall, the lack of oxygen results in cell death. Widespread cell death in the heart results in myocardial infarction, commonly known as a heart attack.

Figure 11.54 Anthracosis of the lung. The black material peppering the pleura of the lung is referred to as anthracosis. This material is mostly comprised of inhaled carbon material. The incised lung shows that the black material permeates the lung. Tobacco smoke is a common cause of anthracosis, and smokers' lungs tend to be laden with anthracotic material. However, because this black material is comprised mostly of carbon particles, there are many other causes of anthracosis. Coal miners and coal furnace workers, for example, can also develop anthracosis.

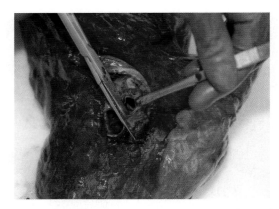

Figure 11.55 Dissection of the pulmonary arteries. Starting at the hilum, or attachment point of the lung, the main bronchi are opened, looking for inflammation and tumors, among other things. The pulmonary arteries and branches are opened, searching for emboli. The lymph nodes at the hilum can be examined at this time as well.

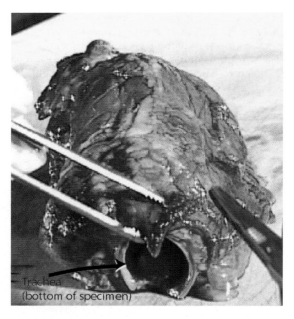

Figure 11.56 Strap muscle dissection. The strap muscles are in the anterior midline of the removed neck organs, and are dissected away. During dissection, the pathologist is looking for hemorrhage.

Some poisons and drugs have unique odors. Cyanide, for example, has the smell of bitter almonds. The sickly fruity smell of ethyl alcohol at autopsy is characteristic. However, one must be cautious in interpreting the odor of alcohol. The author has found that the strength of the odor does not necessarily correlate with the blood level. Also, other compounds, such as acetone,

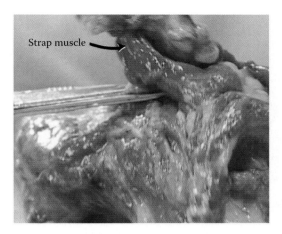

Figure 11.57 Strap muscle dissection. The strap muscles are in the anterior midline of the removed neck organs, and are dissected away. During dissection, the pathologist is looking for hemorrhage.

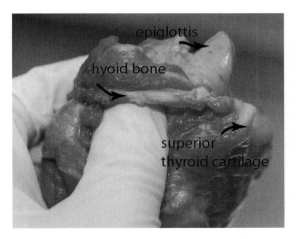

Figure 11.58 Examining the hyoid for injury. The hyoid bone is "cut down on," exposing the periosteum. Fractures of the hyoid bone or hemorrhage of soft tissue around the hyoid bone can be seen in strangulation. The superior thyroid cartilage sticks upward from the thyroid cartilage, and can also show surrounding hemorrhage or fracture in strangulation.

can smell like alcohol. In deaths due to diabetic ketoacidosis, the acetone odor is high.

Specimens to Obtain at Autopsy

Blood

Blood should be saved at all autopsies. Sodium fluoride tubes (or another preservative) should be used if the blood is to be saved any period of time,

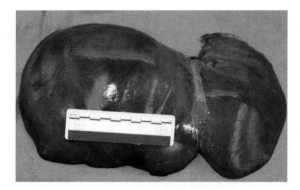

Figure 11.59 Normal liver. The liver is much larger than most autopsy neophytes realize. The liver depicted is about 25 cm (over 10 inches) in width. The average liver weighs about 1930 g (4.5 lb) in a 77-kg (170-lb) man. The liver performs many functions and is essential for life. Important functions of the liver include production of bile; production of blood coagulation proteins; breakdown of drugs and toxins; filtration of blood; and metabolism of fats, proteins, and carbohydrates.

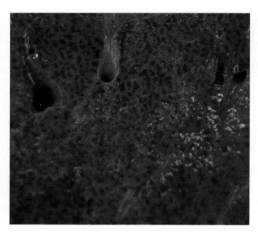

Figure 11.60 Chronic passive congestion of the liver. Close-up of the liver here shows chronic passive congestion of the liver, characterized by alternating light and dark, contrasted areas. This appearance has been called "nutmeg liver" because the cut liver resembles a cut nutmeg. Gross descriptions in pathology occasionally reference food, drinks, and other common objects. The aim of gross descriptions is to communicate observations plainly. The gross appearance reflects the microscopic appearance. The dark areas are largely blood that has pooled around the central vein or "draining area" of blood through the liver.

as it inhibits bacterial growth. At least 20 ml of blood should be obtained; half of this blood should also be placed into plain tubes. Blood is the specimen of choice for alcohol analysis, providing the result in percent, 0.08%, for example, the legal limit for operating a motor vehicle in many states. One must be careful not to use contaminated blood samples. When the stomach

Figure 11.61 Cirrhosis of the liver. The sections of liver shown are very hard. Cirrhosis is simply a scarring of the liver. It is the way the liver reacts to an injury. The injury can be alcohol, an acetaminophen overdose, or chronic ischemia due to heart failure. In cirrhosis, the liver becomes very hard, so that blood cannot flow normally through the liver. This causes the blood to back up elsewhere in the body, such as the esophagus (esophageal varices). Also, the liver begins to fail due to a lack of cells to do the work, such as making clotting factors. As a result, the patient is prone to spontaneous bleeding. A common problem is for a cirrhotic patient to rupture the dilated veins around the esophagus, and clotting is less likely to occur. When advanced, this condition is irreversible and very commonly fatal.

Figure 11.62 Spleen sectioning. On sectioning the spleen, one can see the beet-red, red pulp. The white dots are the white pulp. Red cells pool in the sinusoids of the red pulp. The capsule of the spleen is very thin, making it susceptible to rupture easily with trauma.

is ruptured from a motor vehicle crash, for example, the contents could be admixed with heart blood. When the specific level of a drug is needed, blood concentrations are measured. Drug concentrations can vary, depending on the collection site. In addition to taking heart blood, femoral artery and/or subclavian samples should be taken. At least one tube should be saved for

Figure 11.63 Dissection of the kidney. The kidney is cut along the long axis (shown here), or "bivalved." This type of cut allows a central view of the cortex (blood-filtering glomeruli), medulla (tubules), and calyces (urine-draining portions) of the kidney (see Figure 11.64).

Figure 11.64. Dissection of the kidney. The kidney is cut along the long axis (shown in Figure 11.63), or "bivalved." This type of cut allows a central view of the cortex (blood-filtering glomeruli), medulla (tubules), and calyces (urine-draining portions) of the kidney (shown here).

future testing. In court, the defense might want to have the specimen tested in another lab or new questions might arise over time.

Urine
Urine is the ideal specimen for drug screening. When a drug is detected on the screen, the drug can be quantified in the blood. At least 10 ml should be saved, or ideally 30 to 60 ml. A common problem is that no or very little urine is present at autopsy. In such cases, bladder washings can be performed.

Vitreous Humor
About 2 to 3 ml of clear vitreous fluid can be obtained from each eye and placed in a clean tube. Vitreous fluid is useful in confirming alcohol levels when the contamination of blood is suspected. Drug analysis can be done as

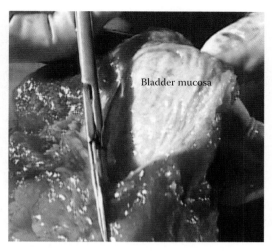

Figure 11.65 Opening the bladder. The dome of the bladder is opened, exposing the pink mucosa below. The urine has been removed.

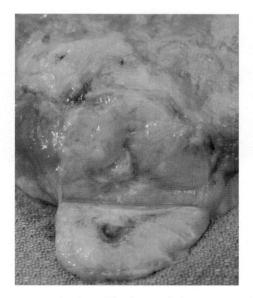

Figure 11.66 Prostate sectioning. The base of the prostate is attached to the bladder. The prostate is serially sectioned. The opening in the cut prostate is the portion of the urethra that courses through the prostate, or the prostatic urethra. The pathologist searches for carcinoma and inflammation.

well. Sodium, chloride, glucose, and blood urea nitrogen (BUN) can be reasonably analyzed as well. Because vitreous glucose decreases after death, the analysis is only helpful in hyperglycemia.

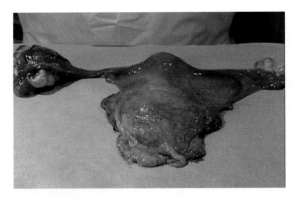

Figure 11.67 Uterus with ovaries and fallopian tubes. The uterus, ovaries, and fallopian tubes are displayed. The large ovary seen on removal can be seen in the left corner of the figure.

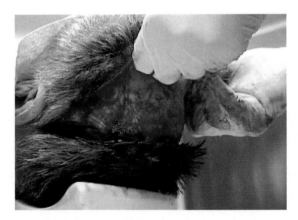

Figure 11.68 Reflecting the scalp back. Once the scalp is reflected back, a scalpel is used to dissect the attached fibrous soft tissue.

Gastric Contents

The stomach is tied off at the duodenum and esophagus for removal. About 50 ml of specimen is ideal. Any pills should be saved. Gastric analysis is very helpful in suicidal overdose cases for establishing intent.

Bile

Bile is useful in cocaine and narcotic analysis. These drugs are concentrated in the bile.

Tissues and Other Specimens

Liver, kidney, brain, heart, muscle, and fat can all be used in toxicologic analysis, especially when no liquid specimens are available. Many drugs are eliminated by the liver or kidneys. These specimens are useful if the deceased

Figure 11.69 Scalp hemorrhage. The scalp is reflected back as the remaining strands of soft tissue are cut. As the scalp is reflected back, a contusion is seen as a darkened area just below the scalpel. The involved soft tissue is cut, showing the underlying contusion hemorrhage.

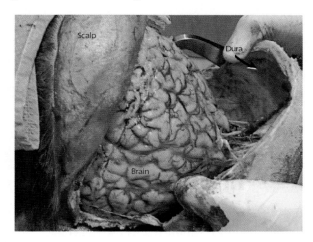

Figure 11.70 Opening the skull. The opened portion of the skull (calvarium) is detached from the base. The pathologist is careful to look for hemorrhage above (epidural) or below (subdural) the dura mater. The dura mater is the tough gray membrane outlined by the arrow.

has been embalmed, decomposed, or if blood is not available. The type of specimen needed for each drug is variable. Consultation with a forensic toxicologist is very helpful before performing the autopsy.

Hair, nails (preferably toenails), bone, and even maggots can be used to detect drugs or poisons. These analyses are to detect the drug (qualitative analysis) and not to determine the quantity of drug. Hair is the best specimen for detecting arsenic poisoning. Also, hair samples can detect chronic drug abuse.

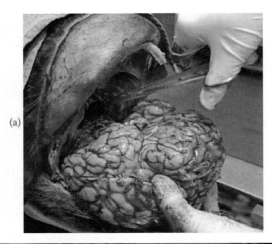

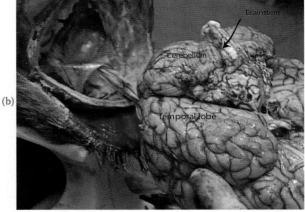

Figure 11.71 Removing the brain. The brainstem is cut (a) and the brain is removed (b).

Finally, all specimens are submitted to the toxicology lab with a chain-of-custody form. This form indicates the type of specimen, the time and date collected, and the signature of the collector. All specimens are sealed with the date, time, and collector's initials written on the seal. All containers are marked with a unique name and case number. The aim of maintaining a chain of custody is to reasonably demonstrate to the court that the results of the analyses are from the person they were taken from.

Certifying the Death

Cause, Mechanism, and Manner of Death

Cause of Death   The *cause of death* is the main disease or injury that begins a decline in the physiology of the vital systems in the body, resulting in death. The *immediate cause of death* is the last major physiologic problem leading to

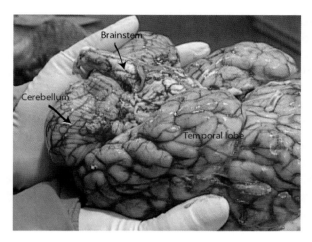

Figure 11.72 Brain upon removal. The exterior of the brain is examined and the brain is weighed. Brain weight is generally 1.4 percent of body weight, or about 1100 g (2.4 lb) in a 77-kg (170-lb) person.

the death. However, the immediate cause of death is always a result of or due to the main disease or injury (cause of death).

For example, a man is walking in a parking lot and slips on the ice, breaking his right hip. He undergoes surgical repair of the hip and is discharged from the hospital. While convalescing at home, he develops swelling in the lower leg. He stands up the next day, and then collapses suddenly. An autopsy shows pulmonary embolus. The *cause of death* is "pulmonary embolus due to fracture of the right hip." The *immediate cause of death* is the "pulmonary embolus." The *manner of death* is "accident." Medical personnel, particularly physicians, are often interested in the immediate cause of death because their focus is on the care of the injury. At times, the cause of death and the immediate cause of death can get confused, and the physician will list "pulmonary embolus" as the cause of death. It is important to understand that the underlying disease or injury that caused the embolus (hip fracture) is the true cause of death.

The cause of death and the immediate cause of death must be linked together both scientifically and temporally. By way of the above example, say the man completely recovered from his fracture without any leg swelling and went back to running marathons for several years. He is then found dead with a pulmonary embolus. The embolus is not temporally or scientifically linked to the hip fracture and one should search for another etiology such as a family history of clots. The link between the cause of death and the immediate cause of death can be complicated and in such cases will take a complete investigation, autopsy, and analysis by a pathologist.

Mechanism of Death   The mechanism of death is the main or last biochemical or physiologic abnormality contributing to the death. There are usually several physiologic abnormalities leading up to death. In the above example, the blood clot blocks the blood from coming out of the right side of the heart, so acute right heart failure and arrhythmia are the two main mechanisms of death. Other common mechanisms of death in MEC cases include shock, exsanguination (bleeding externally), and sepsis (infection of the blood).

Manner of Death   The manner of death is the circumstance surrounding the death. The manner of death must be classified as one of the following: homicide, suicide, accident, natural, or undetermined (cannot be determined is some jurisdictions). See http://www.cdc.gov/nchs/data/dvs/20manual.pdf for more information.

Forensic Experts

12

Introduction

In death investigation, each case is unique and has its own set of questions that must be asked and answered. Sometimes, answering these questions requires specific experts that can add specific knowledge to a case. The death scene investigator (DSI) should be familiar with all types of forensic experts and when a specific expert's opinion might be helpful.

Accident Reconstructionist

These specialists are usually policemen, highway patrolmen, or forensic engineers who have advanced training in recreating motor vehicle crashes. They can estimate the speed of a particular motor vehicle at the time of a crash and predict how vehicles react after impact. They can also determine the location of a person in a vehicle prior to impact.

Forensic Anthropologist

Anthropologists study bones, *that is,* bodies with little or no tissue. They have a better than 90% chance of determining the race, sex, and an age range in most cases. The more complete the skeleton, the greater the accuracy of the determination. With disarticulated skeletons, anthropologists are helpful in determining whether one or more bodies are present (termed "commingling"). Anthropologists are skilled at excavating remains and can be helpful at the scene when skeletal remains are discovered. For example, during recovery, animal bones can be commingled with human bones, or human bones might be missing. Some anthropologists specialize in facial reconstruction, constructing facial detail from skull bones. Unknown skeletons have been identified by this specialized technique. Anthropologists have been known to evaluate specific bony injuries to help with determining cause of death, such as tool marks on bones.

Forensic Botanist

Botanists are able to look at plant material recovered from a scene or body and compare this material to that which is native to the scene. Knowing which plants are indigenous to particular areas helps determine if a body was transported from one location to another. Comparisons can be made with the material associated with a suspect.

Forensic Geologist

Geologists are skilled in the origin of rocks, minerals, and associated soil. This evidence is often transferred if the victim is in contact with the ground or other surfaces associated with geological specimens. As with other evidence that is transferred, comparisons can be made to suspects.

Crime Scene Technician

The job of the crime scene technician begins after the discovery of a body. This expert is a specially trained individual who is usually a member of local law enforcement or a statewide investigative unit. The duties of a crime scene technician vary, depending on the jurisdiction. The technician's expertise includes:

- Photographing and diagramming the death scene
- Collecting all potentially important evidence and trace evidence in an investigation, such as blood, hair, fiber samples, and weapons
- Recovering fingerprints
- Collecting impressions of and photographing patterns such as tire and footwear imprints
- Processing vehicles and other evidence
- Photographing and analyzing blood spatters (if qualified)
- Attending the autopsy to photograph the body and collect further evidence

Criminalist and Criminalistics

Crime laboratories provide services called "criminalistics," usually to large metropolitan areas. The DSI should be familiar with the local crime lab and the services offered. "Criminalist" is a general term for someone who has received training in many different areas, such as questioned documents, ballistics, serology, and toxicology. Most criminalists specialize in one or more fields because each field requires specific knowledge and expertise. Common crime lab services include:

- Fingerprint analysis and interface with AFIS (Automated Fingerprint Identification Systems; see Chapter 8)
- Photography
- Mobile crime scene laboratory
- Firearms analysis, ballistics
- Toxicology
- Serology and biologic fluids
- DNA analysis
- Document analysis or "questioned documents"
- Physical evidence analysis (This expert can test a variety of other materials such as soil for its component elements and glass for its fragility and direction of impact. Footwear impressions and tire treads can be matched with referenced manufacturers and retailers. Paint chips can be analyzed for their components and can be compared to the paint used by known manufacturers. Automobile manufacturers keep accurate records of the paint used on each make and model of their vehicles. Volatile liquids, such as gasoline or paint thinner, can be determined from suspected arson cases.)

Forensic Engineer

Engineers are experts in materials and forces acting upon different materials. Specifically, a forensic engineer has an interest in the interface between his or her expertise and the law. Typically, the engineer is given a problem, such as, Why did the bridge fail? He or she uses experience, research, and/or experiments to render an opinion. Some areas of forensic engineering and examples of expertise include chemical (toxic and explosive chemicals), civil (bridges, roads, and buildings), environmental (natural resources and toxic waste), electrical (electrocutions and electrical fires), and mechanical (faulty controls, devices, and machines) expertise.

Forensic Entomologist

Forensic entomologists are highly trained biological scientists (often Ph.D.-level) whose knowledge includes insect identification and life cycles. These scientists also know how to work with a death investigation team in establishing a postmortem interval and, at times, a cause and manner of death. Forensic entomologists can provide the most reliable estimate of the postmortem interval after 72 hours. The presence of insects on a body is directly related to the location of the body, including geographic location, time of year, and indoors or outdoors, among other factors. Attracted to the decaying body, blow flies and other insects lay eggs or attack and invade the body. Because the life cycle of blow flies and other insects is predictable, a reasonable estimate of the postmortem interval can be established using objective criteria, under the right conditions (such as the body has not been moved, etc.). Ideally, the forensic entomologist should be at the scene to collect larvae and other insect samples. If this is not possible, he or she can come to the autopsy and collect insects directly form the body. It is useful for any DSI to establish a relationship with an entomologist so that even if he or she cannot be present, the DSI knows how to collect specimens at the scene or at the autopsy, for that particular entomologist.

Forensic Pathologist

In the United States, a forensic pathologist is a physician (M.D. or D.O.) who is board certified in pathology and forensic pathology. A pathologist is a physician who specializes in the study of the laboratory diagnosis of disease, such as cancer in a breast biopsy or leukemia in a blood sample. Postmortem examination is also a part of this expertise. A forensic pathologist receives one or more years of additional training in the study of diseases and injuries of the body as it pertains to the courts, law enforcement, and determining the cause and manner of death in the MEC (medical examiner/coroner) system. The training and expertise of the forensic pathologist includes:

- Examining a body at a death scene
- Reviewing medical records for medical and forensic purposes
- Determining the cause of injuries to the body in both the living and deceased
- Performing autopsies for the MEC system
- Acting as a medical examiner or coroner
- Determining when other experts are needed (e.g., toxicology and forensic radiology)

- Identifying and collecting trace and other evidence
- Testifying in court

Forensic Odontologist (Dentist)

A bite mark on a victim or an assailant can be matched to the person making the bite. An odontologist can analyze and interpret this data and is specifically trained to make these determinations. Prior to making molds and photographs of the marks, an odontologist swabs the area to remove any saliva. An offender's blood type can be determined if they are one of the 80% of the population whose blood type is secreted in their bodily fluids. An odontologist is also an important consultant when positive identification is required. Dental comparisons are useful when visual and fingerprint identification cannot be made.

Forensic Radiologist

The expertise of a radiologist is used frequently by an MEC office. Comparisons of antemortem to postmortem radiographs aid in decedent identification. Sinus films, deformities, prosthetic knees, hip, and rods — all can aid in identification. These analyses can be important when a decedent cannot be identified by fingerprints, dental exams, or other means. A radiologist is also consulted for the evaluation of bony injuries or healing rib or leg fractures in cases of suspected child abuse.

Questioned Documents Examiner

These experts are able to analyze handwriting for comparison purposes. They can determine whether or not a suspect actually wrote the document in question. Paper can be analyzed for its ingredients and age, and ink can be analyzed for its chemical composition. Writing instruments, such as typewriters or pens, can also be analyzed.

Serologist

A serologist analyzes fluids removed from a scene: clothing, victim, and/or suspect such as blood, saliva, or semen. The expertise of a serologist includes analysis of blood types (A positive or negative, B positive or negative, AB positive or negative, and O positive or negative), identifying spermatozoa, and processing evidence for DNA analysis. If a specimen from a scene is not decomposed, it can be compared to a blood type of all parties involved in an investigation. Consequently, blood removed from weapons and other objects can be tested. Blood need not be fluid to be of value; dried specimens are still useful. Dried specimens collected at the scene or autopsy are saved in the dry state in an envelope or other paper medium. Plastic bags or other plastic media should not be used. Blood collected at autopsy for serology should be put in an EDTA (purple-top) tube. Many MEC offices retain drops of blood stored on widely available stain cards, which can be placed in an envelope and stored indefinitely. These samples can be useful if there is a future paternity or criminal inquiry requiring the DNA of the deceased. The presence of blood can be confirmed by performing the phenolphthalein test, forming the characteristic deep pink color. Blood can be seen in the luminol test even after attempts have been made to clean it up. At times, on decomposed or inadequate samples, specific typing cannot be performed and a serologist is only able to determine whether or not such blood is human.

Toxicologist

The toxicologist evaluates organs and fluids from an autopsy and a scene for the presence or absence of drugs and chemicals. The types of pills or powders found on suspects can also be determined. Most common drugs of abuse and poisons can be readily discovered and quantitated. However, not every drug and chemical appears in a routine drug screen. The pathologist and investigator must consult with a toxicologist if any unusual drugs or poisons are suspected. They should also let the toxicologist know what prescribed or illegal drugs a decedent was taking. Drugs and medicines from a scene should be recovered for analysis if needed.

Bibliography

Adelson, L.A., *The Pathology of Homicide*, Charles C Thomas Publisher, Springfield, IL, 1974.

Brogdon, B.G., *Forensic Radiology*, CRC Press, Boca Raton, FL, 1998.

Clark, S.C., Ernst, M.F., Haglund, W.D., et al., *Medicolegal Death Investigator*, Occupational Research and Assessment, Inc., 1996.

Collins, K.A. and Hutchins, G.M., *Autopsy Performance and Reporting*, 2nd ed., College of American Pathologists, Chicago, 2003.

Cotran, R.S., Kumar V., and Collins, T., *Robbins Pathologic Basis of Disease*, 7th ed., W.B. Saunders Co., Philadelphia, 2003.

DeGowin, R.L., *Bedside Diagnostic Examination*, 5th ed., MacMillan, New York, 1987.

Di Maio, D.J. and Di Maio, V.J.M., *Forensic Pathology*, Elsevier, New York, 1989.

Di Maio, V.J.M., *Gunshot Wounds, Practical Aspects of Firearms, Ballistics and Forensic Techniques*, Elsevier, New York, 1990.

Di Maio, V.J.M. and Dana, S.E., *Handbook of Forensic Pathology*, 2nd ed., CRC/ Taylor & Francis, Boca Raton, FL, 2006.

Dix, J., *Color Atlas of Forensic Pathology*, CRC Press, Boca Raton, FL, 2000.

Dix, J., *Handbook for Death Scene Investigators*, CRC Press, Boca Raton, FL, 1999.

Dix, J. and Graham, M., *Time of Death, Decomposition and Identification, an Atlas*, CRC Press, Boca Raton, FL, 2000.

Ellenhorn, M.J., *Medical Toxicology, Diagnosis and Treatment of Human Poisoning*, 2nd ed., Elsevier, New York, 1997.

Froede, R.C., Ed., *Handbook of Forensic Pathology*, 2nd ed., College of American Pathologists, Chicago, 2003.

Geberth, V.J., *Practical Homicide Investigation*, 4th ed., CRC/Taylor & Francis, Boca Raton, FL, 2006.

Haglund, W.D. and Sorg, M.H., Eds., *Forensic Taphonomy — The Post Mortem Fate of Human Remains*, CRC Press, Boca Raton, FL, 1996.

Hanzlick, R., *Death Investigation Systems and Procedures*, CRC/Taylor & Francis, Boca Raton, FL, 1997.

Karch, S.B., *The Pathology of Drug Abuse*, CRC Press, Boca Raton, FL, 1993.

Ludwig, J., *Handbook of Autopsy Practice*, 3rd ed., Humana Press, New Jersey, 2002.

Mortiz, A.R., Classical Mistakes in Forensic Pathology, *Am. J. Clin. Pathol.*, 26, 1383, 1956.

Rohen, J.W. and Yokochi, C., *Color Atlas of Anatomy*, 3rd ed., Igaku-Shoin, New York, 1993.

Spitz, W.U., Ed., *Mediolegal Investigation of Death*, 4th ed., Charles C Thomas Publisher, Springfield, IL, 2004.

Stimson, P.G. and Mertz, C.A., Eds., *Forensic Dentistry*, CRC Press, Boca Raton, FL, 1997.

Wagner, S.A., *The Autopsy, Chapter One: Unraveling Life's Mysteries*, videotape, 30 min., Wagner Research, LLC., CRC Press, Boca Raton, FL, 2000.

Wagner, S.A., *Color Atlas of the Autopsy*, CRC Press, Boca Raton, FL, 2004.

Wagner, S.A., et al, Asphyxial Deaths from the Recreational Use of Nitrous Oxide, *J. Forensic Sci.*, 37(4), 1008–1015, 1991.

Wetli, C.V., Mittleman, R.E., and Rao, V.J., *An Atlas of Forensic Pathology*, ASCP Press, Chicago, 1999.

Wetli, C.V., Mittleman, R.E., and Rao, V.J., *Practical Forensic Pathology*, Igaku-Shoin, New York, 1988.

Medical Terminology

A

Acquired: not born with; developed after birth.

Adenoma: a benign tumor made up of glandular elements.

Adhesion: fibrous tissue (scarring) which connects one structure to another as a response to disease or injury.

Alopecia: loss of hair.

Alveoli: air sacs in the lungs.

Ambulatory: able to walk.

Anamnestic: history.

Anastomosis: a joining together.

Aneurysm: an outpouching of a blood vessel or structure.

Angina pectoris: chest pain without death of the heart muscle.

Angiography: an x-ray study of blood vessels by use of dye.

Anoxia: no oxygen.

Antecubital fossa: the space on the arm in front of the elbow.

Antemortem: before death.

Anterior: in front of.

Anthracosis: black pigment from coal or cigarette smoke.

Anthropophagia: insect and animal eating of the body after death.

Arrhythmia: abnormal heart beat.

Arteriolonephrosclerosis: small blood vessel disease of the kidney.

Arteriosclerosis: thickening of artery walls, "hardening of the arteries."

Artery: a blood vessel that takes blood away from the heart.

Ascites: accumulation of fluid in the abdomen.

Asphyxia: lack of oxygen in the blood.

Atelectasis: collapse of a lung.

Atherosclerosis: thickening of artery walls by fatty deposits.

Atrium: one of two chambers in the heart that accepts blood from either the lungs or the rest of the body.

Atrophy: wasting away.

Autolysis: degeneration of cells and tissues after death.

B

Benzoylecognine: a metabolite of cocaine.

Bifurcation: a division into two branches.

Bronchi: the breathing tubes between the trachea and the lungs.

Bronchioles: smaller divisions of the bronchi.

Bronchopneumonia: infection of the lung beginning in the bronchiole (smallest air tube).

C

Calcification: turning hard by the development of calcium.

Cancer: malignant growth.

Capillary: the smallest blood vessel that connects arteries and veins.

Carbohydrates: starches and sugars.

Cardiac: heart.

Cardiac tamponade: blood filling the pericardial sac and compressing the heart.

Cardiomegaly: increased size of the heart.

Cardiorespiratory: heart and lungs.

Cardiovascular: heart and blood vessels.

Cecum: the first part of the large bowel (colon) where the small bowel attaches and the appendix is located.

Cerebral: brain.

Cholecystectomy: surgical removal of the gallbladder.

Cholelithiasis: gallstones.

Chordae tendineae: the strings of tissue connecting the heart valves to the papillary muscles in the heart wall.

Cirrhosis: scarring of the liver from many causes, e.g., alcohol abuse.

Colon: the large bowel, between the small bowel and the anus.

Coma: unresponsive condition.

Congenital: born with.

Congestion: commonly refers to the accumulation of blood.

Conjunctiva: the thin membrane lining the eyelid and eyeball.

Connective tissue: the supporting tissue between structures.

Consolidation: becoming firm.

Contrecoup: opposite the point of impact.

Coronal: the plane across the body from side to side.

Coup: at the point of impact.

Cutaneous: pertaining to the skin.

Cyanosis: the dusky discoloration of the skin due to a lack of oxygen.

Cyst: a hollow structure with a lining that is filled with a liquid or a semi-liquid substance.

D

Decubitus ulcer: an ulcer formed on the skin from pressure.

Dementia: loss of intellectual function.

Dermatome: the distribution of a nerve on the exterior of the body.

Diabetes mellitus: a disease in which the body cannot use sugar because insulin is not being adequately produced by the pancreas.

Diastolic: the lower of the two values in a blood pressure.

Dilated: expanded in size.

Distal: away from the point of insertion.

DNA (deoxyribonucleic acid):   the structural backbone of genetic makeup in chromosomes.

Duodenum: the first part of the small bowel.

Dura mater: the tough, thick membrane located between the brain and the skull.

E

Ecchymoses: hemorrhages beneath the skin (larger than petechiae).

-ectomy: excision of.

Edema: the accumulation of fluid in cells and tissues.

Electrocardioversion: an attempt at cardiopulmonary resuscitation by electrical shock.

Emaciation: generalized wasting away.

Emphysema: lung disease where there is a retention of air because of damage to the alveoli (air sacs).

Endometrium: the inner lining of the uterus.

Epidural: over the dura.

Esophagus: the structure connecting the mouth to the stomach (food pipe).

Etiology: the cause of a disease.

Exsanguination: marked internal or external loss of blood.

F

Fibrillation: very rapid irregular heart beat.

Fibrosis: scarring, commonly associated with liver and the heart.

Flexion: the act of bending a structure.

Foramen magnum: the hole at the base of the skull through which the spinal cord passes.

Forensic pathology: the legal applications to the field of pathology, study of the cause and manner of death and injury.

G

Gastrocnemius: the calf muscle.

Gland: a structure made up of cells that secrete a substance.

Glucose: sugar.

Granular: a "lumpy bumpy" surface.

Granuloma: a tumorlike growth caused by an infection.

H

Hematoma: a mass (collection) of blood.

-hemo: blood.

Hepatic: pertaining to the liver.

Hepatomegaly: increased size of the liver.

Herniation: the protrusion of a structure into another space.

Hyperglycemia: increased sugar (glucose) in the blood.

Hyperplastic: increased number.

Hypertension: high blood pressure.

Hyperthermia: increased body temperature.

Hypertrophy: enlargement.

Hypoglycemia: decreased sugar (glucose) in the blood.

Hypothermia: decreased body temperature.

Hysterectomy: surgical removal of the uterus.

I

Ileum: the third and most distal part of the small bowel.

Infarction: death of tissue from a lack of blood.

Inferior: below.

Inflammation: infection.

Infraorbital: below the eye.

Intercostal: between the ribs.

Interstitial tissue: the supporting tissue within an organ (not the functioning cell).

Intestines: the bowels.

Intima: the innermost structure.

Ischemia: decreased blood flow.

-itis: inflammation.

J

Jaundice: yellow discoloration of the skin from a buildup of bilirubin (a breakdown product of red blood cells) in the body.

Jejunum: the second part of the small bowel.

L

Laparotomy: surgical incision into the abdomen.

Larynx: voice box (contains the vocal cords).

Leukemia: cancer of the blood-forming organs and cells.

Ligament: thick tissue joining bones and cartilage.

Livor mortis: settling of blood after death.

Lumen: the inside of a hollow organ or blood vessel.

Lymph: the clear fluid that drains from the body's tissues.

Lymph node: nodules of tissue along the lymph drainage system.

Lymphoma: cancer of the lymph system.

M

Mastectomy: surgical removal of the breast.

Mastoid: the area of the skull behind the ear.

Media: the middle layer of a blood vessel.

Medial: the middle.

Membrane: the lining tissue within a structure or between two structures.

Meningitis: inflammation of the coverings of the brain.

Mesentery: the structure that supports the intestines.

Metabolite: a breakdown product of a drug or chemical.

Mitral valve: the valve between the left atrium and ventricle in the heart.

Myocardium: heart muscle.

Myocardial infarct: death of the heart muscle from blockage of a coronary artery.

N

Necrosis: degeneration and death of cells and tissues during life.

Neoplasia: tumor or growth.

Nodules: raised skin lesions, may be benign or malignant.

O

Oophorectomy: surgical removal of the ovary.

P

Pancreas: the organ behind the stomach that produces insulin.

Papillary muscles: muscle bundles that control the heart valves.

Parenchyma: the functional tissue of an organ.

Penetration: into a structure.

Perforation: through a structure.

Pericardial sac: the sac surrounding the heart.

Perineum: the area of the body that includes the external genitalia and the anus.

Peritoneal cavity: abdominal cavity.

Peritoneum: the thick tissue lining the abdominal cavity.

Perivascular: around blood vessels.

Petechiae: pinpoint hemorrhages.

Pharynx: the structure at the back of the nose and mouth before the esophagus and larynx.

Pinna: the external ear.

Pleura: lining the lung or inside the chest.

Pleural space: space between the lung and the chest wall.

Posterior: behind or back.

Postmortem: after death.

Prone: lying face down.

Proximal: toward the point of insertion or the main part of the body.

Purging: the decomposed bodily fluids that come out of the nose and mouth.

R

Renal: kidney.

Rigor mortis: stiffening of the muscles after death.

S

Sagittal: a plane across the body from front to back.

Salpingo-oophorectomy: surgical removal of the fallopian tubes and the ovaries.

Sarcoma: a malignant tumor of the soft tissue.

Septicemia: bacteria in the blood system with signs and symptoms of disease.

Shock: inadequate circulating blood volume because of either a loss or redistribution of blood.

Small bowel: the small intestine, extending from the stomach to the colon (large bowel).

Soft tissue: fat or supporting tissue.

Splenectomy: surgical removal of the spleen.

Stenosis: narrowing.

Subarachnoid: beneath the arachnoid.

Subcutaneous marbling: the black discoloration of the blood vessels on the outside of the body that appears during decomposition.

Subdural: beneath the dura

Subluxation: bones that partially slip out of joint.

Superior: above.

Supine: lying on the back with face upward.

Supraorbital: above the eye.

Suture: joints in the skull where the bones come together.

Syncope: fainting.

Systolic: the higher of the two values in a blood pressure.

T

Tachycardia: fast heart beat.

Tardieu spots: small hemorrhages from ruptured blood vessels on the extremities that occur after the body has been in a dependent position.

Thoracic cavity: chest cavity.

Thoracotomy: surgical incision into the chest cavity.

Thorax: chest.

Trachea: (windpipe) the structure between the larynx (voice box) and the bronchi.

Tricuspid valve: the valve between the right atrium and right ventricle in the heart.

U

Ureter: the structure that takes urine from the kidney to the urinary bladder.

V

Varix (Varices):   enlarged dilated vein from a backup of blood , often seen in alcoholics who have cirrhosis of the liver.

Vein: a blood vessel that returns blood to the heart.

Ventricle: a chamber containing either blood or fluid (e.g., the heart has two ventricular chambers).

Vitreous humor: the fluid in the eye that gives the eye its shape.

Source: From Dix, J., *Handbook for the Death Scene Investigator*, CRC Press, Boca Raton, FL, 1999. With permission.

Prescription Medicines

Look up the drug in question alphabetically. The number associated with the drug determines its basic classification. For example: heparin, 3. The "3" indicates heparin is an anticoagulant (a blood thinner). Capitalized drugs are brand names.

Classifications:

1. Analgesic
2. Analgesic (narcotics)
3. Anticoagulant (blood thinners)
4. Anticonvulsant (seizures)
5. Antidepressant
6. Antidiabetic
7. Antiemetic (vomiting)
8. Antihistamine (colds and allergies)
9. Anti-inflammatory (infections)
10. Antineoplastic (cancer)
11. Cardiovascular (heart and blood vessels)
12. Diuretic (fluid removal)
13. Hormone and synthetic substitutes
14. Laxatives and antidiarrheal
15. Miscellaneous and unclassified
16. Muscle relaxant
17. Nervous system, specialized
18. Sedative and hypnotic (sleeping)
19. Tranquilizer
20. Vitamin

A

Abbokinase, 3
acetaminophen, 1
ACTH, 13
Actinomycin D, 10

acyclovir, 9 (viral)
Adenocard, 11
adenosine, 11
Adrenalin, 17
Adriamycin, 10
Advil, 1
albuterol, 17
Aldactone, 12
Aldopa, 11
Alfenta, 2
alfentanil, 2
Alkeran, 10
allopurinol, 15 (gout)
alprazolam, 18
altretamine, 10
Alupent, 15 (lung disease)
amantadine, 15 (viral)
Amidate, 18
amiloride, 12
aminophylline, 16, (also for lung conditions)
aminopyrine, 11
amiodarone, 11
amitriptyline, 5
amlodipine, 11
amobarbital, 18
amoxicillin, 9
Amoxil, 9
Amphocin, 9
amphotericin B, 9 (fungal)
ampicillin, 9
amrinone, 11
amyl nitrite, 11
Amytal, 18
Anafranil, 5
Ancef, 9
Ancobon, 9 (fungal)
Anectine (injection), 16
Antabuse, 15 (used in alcohol withdrawal)
Antivert, 7
Apresoline, 12
Ara-C, 10
ascorbic acid, 20 (C)
asparaginase, 10

Atarax, 1, 18
atenolol, 11
Ativan, 18
Atomid-S, 11
Atracurium (injection), 16
atropine, 17
atropine and diphenoxylate, 14
Augmentin, 9
Aventyl, 5
azathioprine, 10

B

baclofen, 16
Bactrim, 9
BCNU, 10
beclomethasone, 13
Benadryl, 1, 8
Benemid, 15 (gout)
benztropine, 17
betamethasone, 13
bisacodyl, 14
Bismuth, 14
Blenoxane, 10
bleomycin, 10
bretylium, 11
Bretylol, 11
Brevibloc, 11
Brevital, 18
bromocriptine, 15
brompheniramine, 8
Buspar, 18
buspirone, 18
busulfan, 10
butalbital, 18

C

Cafergot, 17 (migraine)
caffeine and ergotamine, 17 (migraine)
calcitriol, 20
Capoten, 11
captopril, 11

D

G

H

L

labetalol, 11
Lactines, 14
lactobacillus, 14
lactulose, 14
Lamprene, 9
Lanoxin, 11
Largon, 1 (antianxiety)
Lariam, 9 (malaria)
Larotid, 9
Lasix, 12
Lescol, 11
leucovorin, 20
Leukeran, 10
leuprolide, 10, 13
levamisole, 15
Levarterenol, 17
Levophed, 17
levothyroxine, 13
lidocaine, 11
lindane, Kwell, 9 (lice)
Lioresal, 16
liothyronine, 13
lisinopril, 11
lithium, 15 (antimaniac)
Lomotil, 14
Loniten, 11
loperamide, 14
Lopressor, 11
loratadine, 8
lorazepam, 18
loxapine, 18
Loxitane, 18
Lupron, 10, 13

M

Macrodantin, 9
magnesium citrate, 14
Magnesium hydroxide, 14
magnesium sulfate, 14
Mandelamine, 9

mannitol, 12
Matulane, 10
Mazicon, 15
Mebaral, 4
mecamylamine, 11
mecaptopurine, 10
mechlorethamine, 10
meclizine, 7
medroxyprogesterone, 13
mefloquine, 9 (malaria)
Megace, 10
megestrol, 10
melphalan, 10
meperidine, 2
mephobarbital, 4
mesna, 15
Mesnex, 15
Metamucil, 14
metaproterenol, 15 (lung disease)
metformin, 6
methadone, 2
methazolamide, 11
methenamine, 9
methimazole, 13
methohexital, 18
methotrexate, 10 (also for psoriasis)
methyldopa, 11
methysergide, 17
metoclopramide, 15
metolazone, 12
metoprolol, 11
MetroGel, 9
metronidazole, 9
Mexate, 10
mexiletine, 11
Mexitil, 11
Micronase, 6
Midamor, 12
midazolam, 18
Midrin, 1
Milk of Magnesia, 14
milrinone, 1
Minocin, 9

N

Q

R

S

U

V

vasopressin, 13
Velban, 10
Ventolin, 16 (lung disorders)
Vepesid, 10
verapamil, 11
Versed, 18
Vicodin, 2
Vibramycin, 9
vinblastine, 10
vincristine, 10
vinorelbine, 10
Vistaril, 1, 18
Voltaren, 1

W, X

warfarin, 3
Wellcovorin, 20
Wycillin, 9
Xanax, 18
Xylocaine, 11

Z

Zantac, 15 (GI)
Zarontin, 4
Zaroxolyn, 12
Zestril, 11
zidovudine, 9 (viral)
Zinecard, 15
Zofran, 7
Zovirax, 9 (viral)
Zyloprim, 15 (gout)

Source: From Dix, J., *Handbook for the Death Scene Investigator,* CRC Press, Boca Raton, FL, 1999. With permission.

Index

A

M